me home. Hometown hero. The chickens have come home to roost. Charity begins at home. Home, home on the range. Bring it on n's place is in the home. This old man came rolling home. I'm gonna pick up my bat and my ball and go home. Retire- home. You'd better watch your happy home. The Lord is calling me home. Celebtrate me home. Mobile home. Homeroom. Home and away we'll go! Welcome home. Hearth and home. Childhood home. Home security system. Old folk's home. See your gal home. at peaches. Go to town and watch the people eat peaches. Mi casa e su casa. Down home. Home front. Home court advantage. Be ne. Don't try this at home. Country home. Second home. Home away from home. Home wrecker. A *Prairie Home Companion*. Home ertainment center. Home pregnancy test kit. Home James, and don't spare the horses. To market, to market, to buy a fat pig – home Home grown. Home run. When the chickens come home to roost. Home is the sailor, home from the sea. Keep the home fires burn- n grass of home. Honey, I'm home! She's leaving home. Sweet Home Alabama. Walkin' my baby back home. Welcome home party. om home. Homemade jam. Homemade clothes. Home fries. Home base. Vacation home. Home birth. Home entertainment center. me again? Hometown. I'll be home for Christmas. Charity begins at home. Eaten out of house and home. Bringing home the bacon. . Bring it on home to me. Home is where the heart is. Drive it home. A man's home is his castle. Nothing to write home about. Old home. Retirement home. The land of the free and the home of the brave. Far from the home I love. Homeowner. You can't go home om. Home from school. Home plate. When Johnnie comes marching home. I'll go home and get my panties, you go home and get gal home. Home free all. Home base. Home office. This little piggy ran whee whee whee all the way home. Don't go home mad. Go tage. Be home soon. The lights are on but nobody's home. Old home week. Home-cooked meal. Home cooking. P-O-S-H: Port out, on. Home grown. Home turf. Home team. Home town advantage. Walk me home. Ma maison. I feel at home here. Make yourself at t pig – home again, home again, jiggity jig. Homecoming. Be it ever so humble, there's no place like home. Home for the holidays. he fires burning. Home improvement. Home is anywhere you hang your hat. Home movies. Bill Bailey, won't you please come home. ome party. You'd be so nice to come home to. Homeward Bound. Look homeward, Angel. Homeboy. Yo, homes! Jesus is my home- ent center. Take the long way home. Homestyle cooking. Welcome home. Homesick. Home port. Home schooled. Home page. Isn't he bacon. 'Til the cows come home. Hometown hero. The chickens have come home to roost. Charity begins at home. Home, home ut. Old home day. A woman's place is in the home. This old man came rolling home. I'm gonna pick up my bat and my ball and go 't go home again. Leaving home. You'd better watch your happy home. The Lord is calling me home. Celebtrate me home. Mobile ne and get your scanties, and away we'll go! Welcome home. Hearth and home. Childhood home. Home security system. Old folk's me mad. Go to town and eat peaches. Go to town and watch the people eat peaches. Mi casa e su casa. Down home. Home front. S-H: Port out, Starboard home. Don't try this at home. Country home. Second home. Home away from home. Home wrecker. A *Prai- ke yourself at home. Home entertainment center. Home pregnancy test kit. Home James, and don't spare the horses. To market, to he holidays. Home economics. Home grown. Home run. When the chickens come home to roost. Home is the sailor, home from the come home. The green, green grass of home. Honey, I'm home! She's leaving home. Sweet Home Alabama. Walkin' my baby s is my homeboy. Run away from home. Homemade jam. Homemade clothes. Home fries. Home base. Vacation home. Home birth. page. Isn't it nice to be home again? Hometown. I'll be home for Christmas. Charity begins at home. Eaten out of house and home. ome, home on the range. Bring it on home to me. Home is where the heart is. Drive it home. A man's home is his castle. Nothing to

at home:
PASADENA

By Jill Alison Ganon & Sandy Gillis
Foreword by David R. Brown

Photography by Jennifer Cheung & Steven Nilsson

Designed by James Barkley

Prospect Park Books

PROSPECT
·PARK·
BOOKS

Published by Prospect Park Books
969 S. Raymond Avenue
Pasadena, California 91105
www.prospectparkbooks.com

Special Sales
Bulk purchase (10+ copies) of *At Home Pasadena* is available to
companies, colleges, organizations, mail-order catalogs and nonprofits
at special discounts, and large orders can be customized to suit
individual needs.
For more information, go to www.prospectparkbooks.com.

Library of Congress Control Number: 2007931682

The following is for reference only:
Ganon, Jill Alison.

Includes index.
ISBN 978-0-9753939-3-2
       1. Pasadena (Calif.)-Architecture.
       2. Pasadena (Calif.)-Interior design.
       Los Angeles (Calif.)-Interior design. I. Ganon, Jill Alison II. Title.

First Edition

Production in the United States of America.
Photographs by Jennifer Cheung & Steven Nilsson.
Design by James Barkley.
Production graphics by Sally Pfeiffer.

Printed in China

I could dance with you until the cows come home.

On second thought, I'd rather dance with the cows until you come home.

– Groucho Marx

Making a Home

By David R. Brown

When Descanso Gardens hosted the forty-third-annual Pasadena Showcase House of Design, it enjoyed a complete makeover of the former home of Descanso's owner, newspaper publisher E. Manchester Boddy. The fundraising brainchild of a group of Pasadena and San Marino women more than 50 years ago, the now-annual Showcase House involves the Herculean and volunteer efforts of dedicated women, the vision and creativity of dozens of interior designers and landscape designers, and the expertise of a small army of volunteer contractors, vendors, antiques dealers, craftsmen, tradesmen and laborers. In the space of just three months, the twenty-two-room, 12,000-square-foot Boddy House and five surrounding gardens were completely transformed in the Hollywood Regency style epitomized by the house's architect, James E. Dolena. Over a one-month period, more than 37,000 people came to see the "new" Boddy House, with the proceeds from ticket sales going directly to the music and education groups long supported by PSHA, with a corresponding boost in both box office and visibility for Descanso Gardens. (*"I had no idea there was such a beautiful place like this in Los Angeles …"* was an oft-overheard comment.)

The experience at Descanso reminded me – again – of how much we like to look inside other people's homes.

At the same time and unbeknownst to me, writers Jill Ganon and Sandy Gillis and photographers Jennifer Cheung and Steven Nilsson were working on this volume – and soon requested to photograph my own home as an example of how one family has made a Pasadena Craftsman-style house into a home over more than twenty years. On the one hand, my wife Judy and I are always hesitant about turning our house inside out. But on the other, it has been a very good home to us, and we have always thought of ourselves as much stewards or curators as owners, happy to have the occasional opportunity to share the many pleasures and lessons this house has brought to our family. Besides, I really do like to peek inside other people's houses, so it seemed only fair to reciprocate.

What we liked about the idea for this book was that it was not about "architecture" or about "historic houses" but about an idea – "home" – and how that freighted and universal concept plays out in a few dozen homes around Pasadena. Of course, we who read and enjoy and collect books like this always take away ideas for our own homes. And, to be truthful, we sometimes are envious of the astonishing range of individuality, care, collecting expertise, aesthetic sensibilities and sensitivity to life, opportunity and surroundings that are found just inside the front doors and behind the hedges and gardens that surround many houses in this town. There is something quite wonderful and rewarding in seeing how other people have made their houses into homes, their buildings and lovingly chosen artifacts into lives. Maybe the pictures also reassure us that we are not the only ones who love our homes the way we do.

Winston Churchill famously quipped, *"We shape our buildings, and then our buildings shape us."* Perhaps the process of "shaping buildings" is what we might recognize, especially through the pictures and text of *At Home Pasadena*, as "making a home." For that is the message most clear to me in these intimate, lovely photographs and caring, perceptive text. "Home" is a reciprocal idea. We as humans make homes, and they in turn shape us, providing not just shelter but the opportunity to make sense out of both the quotidian and the extraordinary in our world. At home, we create a refuge and a place that is uniquely our own – a personal statement of sorts, even if it's made only to ourselves and our family and friends. "Home"… it's impossible even to say the word without breaking into a slow, warm smile.

David R. Brown is the executive director of Descanso Gardens, the former president of Art Center College of Design and a contributor to the book Descanso: An Urban Oasis Revealed, *by Warren Marr (Balcony Press). He and his wife, Judith, live in a Greene & Greene house in Pasadena.*

The Pasadena home

There's No Place Like Home

Most of us have been around long enough to have experienced that certain period in our early semi-adult lives when home was the place you ran into, leaving your keys in the lock, only to search all over for them after scrambling madly to throw on some clean clothes. You had something to do and someone to see, and it was 6 p.m. and you hadn't eaten all day, and the jar of mustard, the wilted celery stalk, and even the bottle of vodka in the freezer were not going to provide you with anything resembling the nourishment you needed to race all over town doing fun, important things. You'd come home at some godforsaken hour, sleep on the unmade bed and wake up the next day to start all over again.

But that changes, usually some time in our late twenties or so, when we begin to understand that, to a certain degree, we are the architects of our fate, and we might as well spool out that fate from within homes that welcome us – that speak to us, as it were. And whether by fate, or luck, or job, or damned good choice, those of us making our homes in Pasadena have a lot of options to consider.

The western expansion of the United States, from its colonial founding through the completion of the first transcontinental railroad in 1869, was all about bringing the civilizing influences of the east to the wild, untamed west. Pasadena's few Victorian and Queen Anne homes attest to that. Yet by the turn of the century, the architectural flow of ideas began to go both ways, as the Pasadena bungalow –

affordable and designed for the manner in which regular Americans wanted to live – followed the tracks of the railways north to Oregon, through the midwest and on to the east coast. Back here in Pasadena, the design of bungalows and other Craftsman-style homes was undertaken by such talented architects as Myron Hunt, Frederick Roehrig, Arthur and Alfred Heineman, Joseph Blick, Louis B. Eastman, and the gifted and prolific Charles and Henry Greene, architects of Pasadena's most beautiful and stately "bungalows": the Blacker and Gamble houses. Nevertheless, the bungalow's deepest roots in Pasadena attest to a desire to provide respectable, modestly gracious living for the working man – a relatively new concept in a relatively new nation.

The 1920s brought great prosperity to the United States and heralded a golden age of architecture in Pasadena. Ours was one of the country's wealthiest cities, benefiting from the work of architects who brought the Mediterranean and European revival styles to the San Gabriel Valley's affable climate and prosperous residents. Among the best known of these architects (who we have not already named) were Sylvanus Marston, Garrett Van Pelt, Edgar Maybury, Cyril Bennett, Roland Coate, Bertram Goodhue, Wallace Neff, Reginald Johnson, Gordon Kauffman – and, of course, Frank Lloyd Wright, whose work was famously, distinctly American.

It is also important to recognize the work of the landscape architects of this period. Kate Sessions had a deep association with San Diego, having designed Balboa Park, but she also imported the jacaranda tree to Southern California, and we

are her beneficiaries in that regard. Famous not only for her gardens, but also for landscapes for such films as *Gone with the Wind* and *Romeo and Juliet*, Florence Yoch designed the grounds for large estates in Pasadena and San Marino, many of them in partnership with Lucile Council. Yoch also worked in west Los Angeles, though historian David Streatfield wrote that she "disliked that fast-living crowd." She worked with many of the architects we listed above, and her gardens were celebrated and much photographed.

The Great Depression saw an architectural slowdown in the United States, though Pasadena was not as hard-hit as some areas, and the wealthy continued to build homes. In the postwar building boom, the famed Case Study Program commissioned architects to experiment with designing affordable, efficient model homes. Such firms as Buff, Straub & Hensman and Kemper Nomland built Case Study homes in Pasadena. Gregory Ain designed twenty-eight Park Planned Homes on Altadena's Highview Avenue, each with the same open floor plan and landscaping by Garrett Eckbo. Richard Neutra, whose architecture embodies the style that we have come to describe as midcentury modern, had worked in Los Angeles since 1925 and designed the Wilkins House (1949) in South Pasadena and the Perkins House (1955) in Pasadena. As the modernists have given way to contemporary architecture, Pasadena is home to Moule & Polyzoides – Architects and Urbanists, whose self-described architectural venture "supports both newness and continuity." Their civic projects, transit villages and housing work to carry our architectural heritage into the future while respecting the past.

So we arrive at the present in a wonderful city that is more architecturally diverse than many realize. While walking the dog on a beautiful spring afternoon, we like to imagine the great Frank Lloyd Wright building his Mayan-influenced La Miniatura in the Prospect Park neighborhood where the Greene brothers already had built some of their most important homes. Oh, to be a bird in the leafy trees, listening to an imagined conversation when Wright and the Greenes – contemporaries, all born within three years of one another – happen to meet. We don't know if it happened, but it could have.

– JAG

Right: A California bungalow serves as the working urban homestead for the Dervaes family's Path to Freedom, their living commitment to a simpler, more ecologically sound lifestyle.

Architect Bob Bennett built this Pasadena house in 1960 for his family. Bob, who designed civic, commercial and residential properties throughout Los Angeles, was the son of Cyril Bennett of Bennett & Haskell Architects, which designed such notable buildings as the Pasadena Civic Center, the Raymond Theater and many commercial properties on Colorado Boulevard. Bob's daughter, Annaly Bennett, is a third-generation architect and an interior designer who lives in her childhood home with her mother, Jean Bennett, her husband, Jared Crawford, and their son, Miles.

As the Architectural Adage Says, "For a Great Building, Get a Great Client"

Think of a movie director (with no musical training) trying to communicate with his music director: *"I want it to be sort of scary sounding, but then feel a little romantic too, because she just knows the boyfriend will show up to save her, but it turns out the boyfriend is a vampire, and there should be a feeling of conflict because somehow the vampire/boyfriend knows he has to save her…."*

The composer has to turn those impressions into music that will satisfy his director. So it goes between architect and client: Turn a series of thoughts and needs expressed by a client into a home.

In this case, the clients were Ender and Catherine Sezgin, and the architect was Aleks Istanbullu, who turned to his wife, Anne Troutman – trained as an architect and particularly skilled at hearing what a client is asking for – to handle the initial meeting with the Sezgins. After describing their needs – how many bedrooms, kitchen essentials, etc. – the only thing Ender and Catherine wanted from their architect was the design and the specifications on the materials, because Ender wanted to be the general contractor.

Here's how Aleks described this happy partnership: *"Ender dealt with the city; he got every permit; he got the foundation guys out there and every other contractor he needed. And if a contractor was not performing to his standard, he just said, 'Fine, let's close out your contract,' and that got everyone's attention, and Ender got the quality he wanted. He took my design and executed it. He did not let go of anything. Every now and again he would come to me and ask, 'How important is this particular detail?' I would give him an honest answer, and he would take care of it, telling me that he would handle the cost question. When it came to materials, he was uncompromising about getting things that were nontoxic and environmentally conscious. By the time he was done, I told him and Catherine they could take over the building aspect of my practice whenever they wanted to."*

Left: Of the hundreds of bungalow courts built in Pasadena in the early part of the 20th century, Reinway Court, designed by Pasadena architect Charles Buchanon in 1916, is among the best preserved of the survivors. The L-shaped, Craftsman-style complex, commissioned by osteopath Henry Rinehart, is now in the hands of the Doe family, who purchased it from Dr. Rinehart's widow, Emma, in 1947. Years of rebuilding and restoring have attracted tenants who have a deep appreciation of the neighborly lifestyle afforded by a Pasadena bungalow court.

Right: Light, space and clean lines at the Sezgin house in Southwest Pasadena.

Opposite, clockwise from top left: The exterior of Matthew White and Thomas Schumacher's penthouse shows off the Spanish and Moorish influences of the Castle Green, designed as a hotel in 1898 by Frederick Roehrig; a 1908 bungalow in South Pasadena is home to Chris Jansen-Gillum and her daughter, Darah; Sally Storch and Ray Turner's Madison Heights colonial revival; Dana Hursey and Jeremy Cowin restored this Gregory Ain Park Planned Home on Highview Avenue in Altadena, built in response to the postwar housing shortage; Garrett Eckbo did the landscaping for the twenty-eight homes, mirroring each other on both sides of the street.

This page, clockwise from above: The historic 1922 Barcelona apartment building in the Playhouse District; a 1924 Spanish colonial revival home, designed by Joseph Kucera and now owned by Fran and Amnon Yariv, sits above the western bank of the Arroyo Seco; the Yarivs' daughter, Gabriela, did the landscaping, designed to set off the home's architecture.

If John Ripley Says It, You Can Believe It

Whittier native and mechanical engineer John Ripley has been an architecture buff since childhood. *"I didn't think I had enough artistic talent to become an architect,"* he says. *"So I did the next best thing and became an engineer."* Around 1980, his interest was further stoked by reading *An Architectural Guidebook to Los Angeles*, the famed work by David Gebhard and Robert Winter; at the same time, John and his wife, Donna, began collecting furniture in the Arts & Crafts style. A stint as a volunteer photographer with a city project to survey Bungalow Heaven pretty much sealed his fate, and he was hooked on Pasadena. In 1983 John and Donna bought a Craftsman home on the outskirts of Bungalow Heaven for both themselves and the period furnishings they'd collected. *"I began researching my street,"* says John, *"and then I went on to other streets. I passed the information I gathered along to the city for its files."*

Before long John realized that his database held perhaps a third of all Craftsman homes built in Pasadena in the early 20th century. So John Ripley, private citizen, decided to complete the list as best he could. Eventually he got in the car and began what he calls a "windshield survey," looking at every address he had and resolving most inconsistencies with good old-fashioned fieldwork. The result is *The Pasadena Houses of the Craftsman Era from 1904 through 1918*, a comprehensive list of all the houses built in that period, and a fantastic tribute to his adopted city.

Since the early 1990s John has used this enormous and quite comprehensive database to help with various historic surveys. The Pasadena Museum of History keeps a printed copy of the database, which includes the year each home was built; the original owner, architect and contractor; the construction cost; the number of stories and rooms; the declared value when built (a casual scan of a single page listed 27 properties built at costs from $900 to $20,000); and the value per room. It is a fascinating document, and a most remarkable accomplishment.

Tim Gregory: Building Biographer

What started as a hobby has become Tim Gregory's full-time job: a historian of homes. For realtors and curious homeowners, he researches documents, historic resources, previous owners, architects and builders to develop a comprehensive history. He started out with homes in Pasadena, South Pasadena and San Marino but now covers all of Los Angeles County. His business keeps him plenty busy, and he doesn't have (or need, he says) a web site, but he can be reached at timgregory@sbcglobal.net. Consider this: A house bio makes a fantastic housewarming or birthday gift.

Left: A glazed-tile water feature provides serenity in the area between the house and garage in a compact Gregory Ain-designed home in Altadena.

Below: These vents in the Wilkins House have been restored to their thoughtful function, essential to a Richard Neutra design: the merging of the outdoors with a home's interior. Closed, the vent looks like a paneled section of the wall; when opened, the ingenious screened and louvered ventilation system allows air to circulate without need for opening a window, which would have required a screen that would compromise the view of the outdoors. Current owners Stacey and Jeff Mann were delighted to discover these vents. *"We didn't know what they were or even that they were there – the wall panels had been screwed shut, so they were completely nonfunctional,"* says Stacey. *"So we replaced all the hinges, got hardware and rebuilt the screens. Now everyone who comes into the house is drawn to them. We sleep with the bedroom vents open – they work perfectly."*

This page: Richard Neutra's 1949 Wilkins House in South Pasadena, now owned by Stacey and Jeff Mann; note the sliding glass wall, which extends the entertaining and living area to the outdoor terrace.

17

Left: Wallace Neff designed this home in 1931 for Clark B. Millikan, son of Caltech founder Robert A. Millikan. The gated hacienda on 2.5 acres is said to have been one of the architect's favorite projects. Neff, who designed Pickfair, the home of Mary Pickford and Douglas Fairbanks, also designed the dome-shaped1946 Shell House in Pasadena as an experiment in affordable housing.

This page, top: Margie Simpson designed this home in the colonial revival style on a property situated across from Sierra Madre's Bailey Canyon, with backyard views of the beautiful San Gabriel Valley.

Above left: Spanish jasmine grows along the fence outside Christine Madsen and Steve Perry's 1904 Indiana farmhouse in southwest Pasadena; it was designed by Joseph Blick, who designed many homes in Pasadena and is remembered for the 1924 Scottish Rite Cathedral on Pasadena's Madison Avenue.

Above right: Classic California outdoor living at Milo Reice and Carol Chenowith's California ranch house.

Right: The Pasadena-based firm Moule & Polyzoides has created much-lauded civic and residential architecture, including Mission Meridian, a mixed-use project adjacent to the Gold Line stop in South Pasadena. It blends seamlessly but with great energy into an established mixed commercial and residential neighborhood, comprising non-chain retail stores, courtyard lofts, Craftsman-style duplexes, single-family homes and below-street parking.

Opposite page: Anne and Neal Dougherty's Altadena home was originally built in 1912 as a three-story chalet (called Boulder Crest, for obvious reasons) for Los Angeles haberdasher and patron of the arts Reinhardt Busch (no relation to Adolphus of Pasadena's famed Busch Gardens) but was destroyed in the 1935 Los Flores fire. Commencing in 1946, and continuing for seven years, student protégés of Frank Lloyd Wright designed and built a home for then-owners Harold and Dorothy Foote within the footprint of the home's original stone foundation. The Doughertys purchased the home from the Footes in 1972.

This page, clockwise from top: The Babcocks have lived on a quiet cul-de-sac in their Lacy Park neighborhood for forty years, the last ten in this lovely home; the developers of the north end of the Prospect Park tract built this Sylvanus Marston house in 1913 as a model home to entice buyers to the new neighborhood, and today it is owned by Sam and Bettyrae Eisenstein; this English country-style shingled home in Linda Vista was designed by J. Constantine Hillman in 1916; originally a schoolhouse built in1888 (opposite the current Linda Vista School), this building was later purchased as a guest cottage and moved to its current location in the same neighborhood.

National Register Districts

Arroyo Terrace
Lower Arroyo Seco
Old Pasadena
Orange Heights – Barnhart
Pasadena Civic Center
Pasadena Playhouse
Prospect Boulevard
South Marengo Avenue

Local Landmark Districts

Banbury Oaks
Bungalow Heaven
Crawford's Vista
Garfield Heights
Governor Markham
Holliston Avenue
Normandie Heights
Ross Grove
South Oakland Avenue
Washington Square

Opposite page, far left: Bertram Goodhue, architect of the 1926 Los Angeles Public Library, designed *mi sueño*, a Spanish colonial revival home in 1915 for east coast financier Herbert Coppell, as well as created the buildings for the Panama-California Exposition at San Diego's Balboa Park. Goodhue's only residence in Pasadena, the Coppell House retains 10,000 square feet of its original 16,000, having been divided at its grand entry hall in a 1950s attempt at preservation. The smaller 6,000-square-foot home has been preserved and stands next door. In 1998, Norma and Gary Cowles purchased this home, which was in a state of extreme disrepair, from "Wall of Sound" music producer Phil Spector, and spent three years conducting an impeccable remodel and restoration.

Opposite page, right: A San Marino Italian revival, built in 1924 by Weston & Weston; Italian influence seen in clipped boxwood garden, roses and pedestal urns.

Right: Adena Mansion, a city landmark and the oldest home in the historic Garfield Heights neighborhood, was built circa 1887 in a blend of Victorian styles, with Queen Anne and Italianate claiming the most obvious pedigree; it was meticulously restored by Mark Puopolo and Chris Mullen.

Opposite page: The 1907 Mary Ranney House is one of a cluster of Greene & Greene homes built on Arroyo Terrace from 1901 to 1907. Ranney, founder of Westridge School in 1913, was a draftsman for Charles and Henry Greene; scholar Randall Makinson said she was *"given the opportunity to develop much of the design for her own house."* Owners David and Judith Brown purchased the house in 1985 from Nancy and Dennis Kailey, who had restored the run-down property with a group of partners. As there were no outdoor light fixtures, some members of the restoration team designed lamps – an experience that inspired them to start the Arroyo Craftsman lighting company.

This page: Now owned by Liza Kerrigan and built as a summer getaway by John Dupre in 1918, the Sturtevant House property originally consisted of ten lots containing numerous fruit trees, including fig, guava, olive and almond. An advertisement for its sale proclaimed, *"Architect's beautiful home in Sierra Madre foothills, second healthiest place in the world. 1,500 foot elevation, frostless; unsurpassed views of San Gabriel Valley, Catalina Island and Mount Jacinto. Well-built Swiss chalet; large boulder fireplace modeled after medieval fireplace in Scotland."* The home and three lots were sold in the early 1920s for $16,000.

25

Make Yourself:
at home

Tell me what company you keep, and I'll tell you what you are.
— Miguel de Cervantes, *Don Quixote de la Mancha*

Good company and good discourse are the very sinews of virtue.

— Izaak Walton, *The Compleat Angler*

Rinse not your mouth in the presence of others.
— *Rules of Civility and Decent Behaviour in Company and Conversation*

A tiny girl asked her mother, *"Are there witches in our world?"* Her mother reassured, *"No, dear, only in storybooks. And Broadway musicals."* Parsing society's social orders and hospitality is serious business for little children, but, thankfully, it's easier for those of us who accept a dinner invitation at a friend's house. Storybook witches are, of course, a metaphor for the perils that await at every turn, just as magical fairies illuminate possible wonders and happiness on the path ahead. And although neither witch nor fairy live among us, from time to time it would be convenient to believe they are here. During the holiday rush, for instance, when you go to pick up a fabulous Christmas log at Europane, and you must wait in a line that is twenty-seven deep. You wait patiently for your turn and then they can't find your order, so you struggle not to become a wee bit impatient, which makes them search harder, but they still can't find it. They look through the stack of holiday orders, because in the hubbub you forgot your receipt and there, plain as day, is your order! Which shows you're a day early. At that moment you are one of the witches who does not live in our world. The counter girl was so composed and courteous, even though she was well within her rights to hiss. Which means that Counter Girl was some kind of holiday sprite.

Back to those who charm with capability and generosity. If you were lucky as a child, you were fêted in households other than your own, encouraged to relax, kick back and make yourself at home. Your playmate down the block welcomed your Midge into her Barbie's Dream House and provided you with good snacks. Or your Auntie made you fluffy pimento-cheese sandwiches and sweetened tea for lunch and let you watch Mike Douglas with her while she ironed. Through social interactions with family and friends, by way of school, cotillion and Jack and Jill, we learn to be good guests, which includes exhibiting good behavior while visiting. For even though Auntie hugs and loves us no matter what, Mom still gives us the list of dos and don'ts so we will be invited back. So that they, too, might be invited back, 18th-century youngsters hand-copied the "Rules of Civility & Decent Behaviour In Company and Conversation" to reinforce acceptable manners. These guidelines paved the way for Emily Post and still apply: *"Make no Shew of taking great Delight in your Victuals, Feed not with Greediness, Cut your Bread with a Knife, lean not on the Table neither find fault with what you Eat,"* and *"If others talk at Table be attentive but talk not with Meat in your Mouth."*

So you're all grown up, you don't talk with your mouth full of meat, and you're settled into a home and a town with people you're lucky enough to call friends. You may notice a happy spell cast on you several times a year, or more often if you're paying attention. Recognizing you're in good company is half the battle, so stay alert at that luncheon or dinner party or holiday celebration, even if you expected it to be an onerous obligation. It just might turn out to be charming or unexpectedly crazy fun or even one of the most memorable evenings you've spent since you started eating solid foods. Good times have a pleasant way of sneaking up on us, like a wad of dollars found in a pocket on laundry day. Or Tuesday-night tickets to the Pasadena Playhouse and the discovery that Jerome, Zev and Esther are two rows behind you, and it's been over a year since you've seen each other, which calls for a drink after the show! Or at the block party, when your glass of pink lemonade reflects the fiery sunset you share with your neighbors. The witches and fairies will leave you be, but only if you accept and extend invitations once in a while. Pretty soon you'll be in a home among friends, laughing so hard at a silly joke that even Emily Post would look the other way when your beverage comes out of your nose. Which means you've made yourself at home.

– SG

Clockwise from upper right: The living room in Heather and Harvey Lenkin's home on the banks of the Arroyo; the dining room in Sam and Betty Eisenstein's Sylvanus Marston home; Bob Kneisel lights a fire when company comes to his bungalow; Jane Hermann's teacups.

Mediterranean in the Dining Room, Japanese in the Kitchen

Norma and Gary Cowles are busy people. And they like it that way. Still, they frequently make time to fold friends into their schedules, often by hosting them overnight. *"We have guests with us about one week out of every month,"* says Norma. *"Of course, over the holidays, it might be a little busier than that."* But who's counting? Friends and family can function with autonomy in the Cowleses' guest suite, which features a kitchenette, a giant-screen TV with surround sound, and commodious sleeping room for a family of four. *"It's a very comfortable set of rooms,"* says Norma. *"And we use it as a study when no one's staying here."*

With or without sleepovers, Norma and Gary entertain several nights a week. *"The formal dining room is constantly in use,"* says Norma. She's the cook, although Gary loves to have guests. *"It's too noisy when we go out, and we so enjoy having people over,"* she says. *"I cook whatever's simple. Mediterranean meals in the dining room, like paella or osso buco. My favorite meal? I make Japanese food in the kitchen. It's less formal, and it's fun."*

This page: The public spaces in the Cowles house are both grand and comfortably inviting.

29

The Gang's All Here

The street is misleading, as so many are in Altadena. What looks like an undeveloped canyon turns out to be a corner piece of early-20th-century farm property. This leads down a narrow lane of modest midcentury homes, at the end of which are wrought-iron gates opening to a grand driveway. A turnabout is delineated by a cluster of mature Japanese maples and shaded by a redwood grove, uncommon here in deodar land. Welcome to Paul and Julie Thomson's home.

The Thomsons converted their four-car garage into a home gym when they bought this Mediterranean manor several years ago. Not to worry – the driveway holds nine large cars easily, and it often does. *"In the spring, when we have a little more daylight but it's still cool in the evening, we have tennis dinners,"* says Julie. *"Those who don't play tennis still like to eat, so everybody wins."* Julie grew up in a large, Western family, where church socials and community service were weekly events. Cooking for a crowd is the way she learned to run a kitchen. *"Plus, I had waitressing jobs all through college, so carrying lots of plates seems natural to me. I might fall over if I didn't have at least four plates for balance."*

Paul was reared in Wales, in a convivial small town where everyone knew everyone else. He moved away for university where he played rugby, always enjoying the requisite rugby pint with his mates. Later, Paul made lifelong friends with other ex-pats working in Caracas, and he still sees them annually. *"I meet up with my mates at car races around the world,"* says Paul. *"I highly recommend it as a solid way to keep in touch with old friends. Unless Julie's planned a party, that is. I don't want to miss out here."* Paul mans the barbecue, cooking twice a week for friends and family. *"Tri-tip and chicken breasts are his specialties,"* says Julie. *"We like simple, clean food."* Weekend dinners include eight to twelve friends in the dining room, or a larger group for an alfresco meal on the patio.

During the week, dinners might be leftovers or vegetables and hors d'oeuvres, which can be assembled quickly. Unless they're at football or volleyball practice, teenage sons Brady and Gavin are present, whether it's a party or just a family dinner. *"Most of our friends still have children at home,"* says Julie. *"So it's unusual to have fewer than four teenagers at the table with us."* Several friends like to try new recipes, and Julie's test kitchen is the place. Many bring a starter course or dessert. *"I'm not even sure how that tradition started,"* says Julie. *"When the kids were small, a lot of our friends were working, and it was easier to assemble a meal if you only had to worry about one or two elements instead of a five-course dinner. Easy makes it fun for everyone. And getting together is the most important thing, so it must be manageable or people won't enjoy themselves. And if they don't enjoy themselves, well, let's fix that."*

For special occasions, such as team parties or school functions, Julie calls the Taco Lady. Maria Teresa Villalvaso brings all the ingredients for soft tacos, including three kinds of seasoned meats, guacamole, rice, beans, salsas to put hair on your chest or take it off, and chopped radishes, onion and cilantro. The meats are cooked on a grill, tortillas heated to order, and her steaming, fragrant tacos disappear at a frightening rate. *"Brady always asks me to order more food from Teresa than we need,"* Julie says. *"We freeze it so he can eat it later, when he needs a Teresa boost."*

This page, clockwise from upper left: Friends gather in the cool of the Thomsons' covered patio; Maria Teresa Villalvaso, aka the Taco Lady; Julia Katz, Kate Herrill and Camille Katz make quick work of Teresa's tacos; guests (left to right) Beverly Katz, Maryanne Herrill and Stephanie Miller; hosts Paul and Julie Thomson, left, with friend Bob Cunningham.

Opposite page: Scenes from a Mexican-food fiesta at the Thomsons' house, including Stephanie Miller putting the final touches on the table, which is set up in the living room for larger dinner parties.

Vineyard Socials

When Ann Cutting and Tom Soulanille bought their 1895 Arroyo property (right) a funny thing happened: They became farmers. First they fell in love with the three-story shingled house with six bedrooms and five baths, and then they had to deal with the backyard, comprised mainly of a vineyard that the previous owners had planted. Not knowing a thing about growing or harvesting grapes, Ann and Tom decided to give it a try. *"They taught us how to do everything,"* Ann says of the previous owners. *"And we've had good yields over the last four years. It's been trial and error but we've produced some good wines: sangiovese, cabernet sauvignon, malbec. We only use what we grow – no supplementing with other harvests."*

After several years, Ann, Tom and their two sons are fixtures in the neighborhood. For the first few years, they walked with their boys to the nearby preschool every day. And now, when it's harvest time, they put out an all-call to neighbors and friends. *"We invite everyone over to harvest,"* says Ann. *"The boys invite their friends. They especially love the de-stemming machine."* The harvest begins early in the morning with Ann's breakfast and coffee to fuel the laborers, and continues all day. *"We feed everyone dinner, finishing up with last year's wine and cheese for dessert."* Ann has commissioned labels for their homegrown wine. Says the girl from Marblehead, Massachusetts: *"We're going to stay here for a long time."*

Besides becoming farmers, Ann and Tom have a considerable task just taking care of this 19th-century jewel. *"Yes, there's always something to be done, replaced, repainted,"* says Ann. *"We're restoring instead of remodeling."* The latest endeavor was extending the big wrap-around porch, which meant losing a large bay window in the living room. *"As we took out the window, we found stone columns inside the wall,"* says Ann. Without having the original plans, they ended up unintentionally (and serendipitously) restoring the original footprint of the living room, which they later confirmed with an old *Ladies' Home Journal* they found in the house. A photograph in the magazine showed the living room as it was when it was built, with a bigger front porch – exactly what Ann and Tom had in mind. *"We discovered that the living room had been pushed out in the 1920s,"* says Ann. *"Now it's cozier, and we have the same amount of light. It's just what we wanted."* And this bigger porch is the favored spot for relaxing at the end of the day – and, even better, having neighbors over for wine and cheese.

Rules of Civility and Decent Behaviour in Company and Conversation

Every action done in company ought to be with some sign of respect to those that are present.

Shew nothing to your friend that may affright him.

In the presence of others, sing not to your self with a humming noise, nor drum with your fingers or feet.

Spit not in the Fire, nor Stoop low before it neither Put your Hands into the Flames to warm them, nor set your feet upon the fire especially if there be meat before it.

Shift not yourself in the Sight of others nor gnaw your nails.

Kill no vermin as Fleas, lice, ticks, etc., in the sight of others, if you see any filth or thick Spittle put your foot Dexteriously upon it if it be upon the Cloths of your Companions, Put it off privately, and if it be upon your own Cloths return Thanks to him who puts it off.

Do not puff up the cheeks, loll not out the tongue, rub the Hands or beard, thrust out the lips, or bite them or keep the Lips too open or too Close.

Let your Countenance be pleasant but in Serious Matters Somewhat grave.

Keep your nails clean and short, also your hands and teeth clean yet without shewing any great concern for them.

In visiting the sick, do no presently play the physician if you not be knowing therein.

Be not hasty to believe flying reports to the disparagement of any.

Be not immodest in urging your friends to discover a secret.

Eat not in the streets, nor in the house, out of season.

Take no Salt or cut Bread with your knife Greasy.

Labour to keep alive in your Breast that Little Spark of Celestial fire Called Conscience.

In with the In Crowd

At the Bennett house in Pasadena, the "in" crowd gathers around the conversation pit, which Bob Bennett included in the home he designed for his family in 1960. One can draw a line from Richard Neutra's focus on bringing the outdoors into his 1940s designs to the Bennett's conversation pit, which sits in a spacious patio, enclosed by floor-to-ceiling glass and sliding-glass doors, with the backyard swimming pool just beyond. These original aqua vinyl cushion covers are a perfect match to Bob Bennett's 1955 Thunderbird, which is still in the family's possession.

Annaly remembers countless parties her parents hosted when she was a little girl in the swinging '60s. Especially exciting and glamorous to 5-year-old Annaly was the time her parents had just returned from a big European trip. They festooned the house with TWA posters beckoning travelers to Italy, Germany and France and, dressed as a French waiter and waitress (with Mom in fishnet stockings), served their guests baguettes and French wine. Then there was a magical Mexican party with a mariachi band that serenaded 6-year-old Annaly to sleep outside her bedroom window. In junior high and high school, Annaly and her friends took over the conversation pit, spinning Elton John records into the wee hours. Nowadays, mother and daughter still kick up their heels in the Bennett living room.

This page, top: Clean lines and simple adornments mark this 1960s classic; bottom: walls of glass bring the outdoors into this enclosed patio.

Opposite: Scenes from a Bennett gathering; around the conversation pit, clockwise from left, are Annaly Bennett, her mother, Jean Bennett, her husband, Jared Crawford, friends Milo Reice and Carol Chenowith, son Miles Crawford and friend Mark Williamson.

They Captured the Castle

We were fortunate to get to tour the penthouse in the Castle Green before owners Matthew White and Thomas Schumacher moved to New York. Thomas is a Broadway producer (*The Lion King*), and Matthew is a nationally known interior designer who also has a product line of decorative artifacts. He is also a traveler and a collector, with a keen eye for antiquities both serious and whimsical, as well as a gracious host. During their three-year residence at the Castle Green, Matthew and Thomas spent enormous amounts of time and money restoring the only rooftop garden apartment at the Castle Green.

Designed by Frederick Roehrig and built in 1898, this was Pasadena's first fireproof building with structural steel framing, and it's the only early-Pasadena hotel to have survived into the 21st century. Originally, the Moorish-accented penthouse featured a glass ceiling, which was long gone when Matthew and Thomas began their restoration. Modern building codes made it prohibitive to re-create the original, but while searching for structural beams under layers of plaster, Matthew excavated steel girders stamped "Carnegie," manufactured before the steel company was sold in 1901. Now exposed and polished, these load-bearing supports are a striking focal point in the grand salon, a light-filled, multi-function room. By day it served as Matthew's office, with a desk that converted into a dining table for frequent dinner parties. The couple entertained here often, taking care to creatively manage public and private quarters in this home without walls. Storage happens. By design, convertible pedestals serve double duty as art display stands and secret storage compartments. A wall hutch looks like an entertainment center but is actually a fabulous oversize closet. When no one was looking, we peeked inside. *"I would have done the same thing,"* said Matthew, adding, *"Was it tidy?"* Remarkably so, for being two stories tall and requiring a rolling library ladder to reach the sweaters on the top shelf. The kitchen is compact and shipshape, with a casement window that opens for balmy rooftop breezes and eastern sunrises.

This page: Inside the Castle Green penthouse apartment.

Opposite page: Above Pasadena on the Castle Green rooftop terrace.

Cooking & Eating:
at home

If we are house-proud here in Pasadena, we are simply out of this world when it comes to our kitchens. Some are small and marvels of efficiency, with four or forty people fed from one modest space – *My goodness, how does she do it? And a Christmas goose this year, no less!* Some are large and luxurious or devastatingly sleek. We make cupcakes with our children in these sunny rooms and remember our mothers and grandmothers in their tiny, hot kitchens, where we watched and helped and kind of understood that someone cared about what we ate. Or maybe Mom couldn't cook to save her life, and we recall the housekeeper who came on Fridays and always prepared a roast with strict instructions for Mom to take it out of the oven the moment the timer went off, and we can still picture those often-charred roasts that were never removed in time. We assemble books filled with pictures from the scores of shelter magazines devoted to kitchens; we pass untold hours studying appliances, energy-saving devices and that gorgeous cappuccino maker that could just as well be on the counter in your favorite *barra* in Firenze. We Pasadenans have our own restaurant-supply store that welcomes home chefs (thank you, Bob Smith), as well as the California School of Culinary Arts and a host of exceptional architects and kitchen designers. Let's face it, dude – we are *gone* on kitchens.

It's a good thing that we adore our kitchens, because we tend to live in them. (And given that this is Los Angeles, it is not unusual for our kids to recognize their friend's kitchen in a TV commercial.) Homework gets done, calendars are hung and then filled with scheduled soccer games, fundraisers and

orthodontist appointments, laundry is folded, gossip is traded, little kids tell their first jokes, and bigger kids hang out with their big friends, always ready to eat. Everyone, in fact, comes to the kitchen to eat, preferably with gusto. Let's be honest – most of us are distrustful of the eat-to-live types who will never nod off dreaming up a way to use the four varieties of onions they're growing and who have never known the joys of a frozen Milky Way… damn them and their washboard abs anyway.

So with all this quality eating to be done, at least one member of the family tends to cook. And we don't mean opening a few bags of frozen this 'n' that from our beloved Trader Joe's. We mean cook. On top of that, our temperate climate allows us to grow year-round kitchen gardens, and many Pasadenans do just that – for it is, ultimately, the quality of the ingredients that governs the quality of the food we prepare. Pasadena has two weekly farmer's markets; South Pasadena has one; and at least half a dozen others take place in the surrounding towns. And we have a populace and an economy that supports good markets and plenty of specialty food and wine stores.

Okay, we admit it – sometimes we spend so much money creating, remodeling or restoring our fantabulous kitchens that we'd never dare whisper the cost to that grandmother at whose side we learned to crack eggshells with one hand. She would be shocked – but she would also be thrilled that we still make her creamy rice pudding because our kids love it, as much as they love hearing the tale of the time we surprised her by adding full bottles of red and blue food coloring to the rice pudding

cooling in the fridge for her bridge ladies later that afternoon.

Our kitchens are Mom's roast chicken, Abuelita's chile verde, Dad's Sunday kippers and eggs, and our son's first batch of chocolate-chip cookies. Whether there's a fireplace there or not, the kitchen is the hearth of our home.

– JAG

Kids in the Kitchen

Catherine and Ender Sezgin want their children to grow up enjoying fresh, healthy foods; their philosophy, says Catherine, is, *"If they're old enough, and it's safe enough, they can prepare it."* Her pragmatic approach recognizes that when children learn to cook food, they typically have more interest in eating it. Evren, 9, and Erin Sibel, 7, are not yet of an age where they can safely use the stove or oven without supervision, but Catherine describes herself as a great delegator. *"Otherwise,"* she says, *"you can prepare something, and it is like they are at some restaurant they're not paying for. What is that?"*

The combination of world travel with their parents and a personal involvement in cooking has expanded the palates of these young chefs. Catherine loves cookbooks and magazines, but, she says, *"I'm not a domestic goddess, sacrificing myself for my family. If they want to eat, they should join us in the kitchen. Cooking here is not a perfectionist operation."* She describes those kitchen glitches – that clunking sound in the food processor that turned out to be the missing aluminum knob – as part of the process and part of the fun. Ender is Turkish, so the family cooks a lot of Turkish food; when they go out, they enjoy the good local Armenian and Persian restaurants. Evren and Erin Sibel are currently mad for baking cupcakes, and their mother tells us it was a revelation for them to realize that such confections could be made from scratch.

Catherine is philosophical about the need for give and take when it comes to educating children about food. She says it sometimes makes her a little sad when they pass a Burger King and her children offer up the family propaganda about junk food, when deep down she believes that, really, they might love to drop in for a bite. So there is compromise – as is the case for so many families in these parts, they make the occasional visit to In-N-Out.

A Modified Galley Kitchen

An important focal point of the Sezgin house in Southwest Pasadena is its backyard, and it was imperative, especially when the children were younger, that whoever was cooking could watch the kids in the yard. The home's architect, Aleks Istanbullu, says the kitchen table is his favorite part of the house, and Catherine agrees: *"I love to sit at the table, where the light is great and you have wonderful views of the house. It is the true center of our home."* She describes her *"scaled-down"* kitchen as being influenced by Istanbullu's European aesthetic. There is a lot of open space, and the compact work area allows the cook to take food from the refrigerator and set it right on the adjacent prep counter next to the Thermador stove, where there's easy access to the sink. They also created a breakfast (or quick lunch) area comprising cupboard, additional sink and countertop. There was some discussion of an island, but not at the cost of a kitchen table, which was of paramount importance to the family. *"The eating-together philosophy that we'd grown up with,"* says Catherine, *"was what we wanted."*

Cooking a Kitchen – From Scratch

The beautiful 1911 hunting lodge in Eagle Rock that is now the home of Joseph Shuldiner and his partner, Bruce Schwartz, had great bones, as they say, but the interior needed what Shuldiner calls *"a loving restoration,"* and that is precisely what it received. As for the kitchen, they decided to gut the entire thing (including a porch area) and start from scratch. They had a tear-sheet book of images they'd been collecting for years, and an architect friend helped them create a plan. They decided where all the appliances would go and chose the materials (including mahogany counters) and colors.

Shuldiner is the household cook. *"We're pretty healthy eaters,"* he says. *"We were vegan at one point, but now we call ourselves 'vaguely vegetarian.'"* Shuldiner likes to cook gourmet dishes that he alters to suit their palates and health-consciousness – like the following lasagna. Carb-watchers, don't panic – mandoline-sliced zucchini ribbons fill in for the pasta.

Above: Joseph Shuldiner and Bruce Schwartz's Eagle Rock home was built as a hunting lodge, which is evident in their dining room.

Right page: Scenes from the Shuldiner/Schwartz kitchen.

Zucchini & Roasted Tomato Lasagna with Walnut-Basil Pesto

Serves 6

4 medium zucchini, ends trimmed
2 pints ricotta cheese
1 egg, lightly beaten
1/2 tsp. sea salt
1/2 tsp. freshly ground pepper
Olive oil
Tomato Sauce (see recipe below)
Walnut-Basil Pesto (see recipe below)
Roasted Tomatoes (see recipes below)
1 lb. mozzarella cheese, grated

Heat oven to 350 degrees. Shave zucchini lengthwise into very thin slices on mandoline and set aside.

Mix together ricotta, egg, salt and pepper in medium bowl until just incorporated, cover with plastic wrap and set aside.

Line bottom of 9-by-13-inch baking dish with two layers of zucchini slices. Brush zucchini lightly with olive oil, spread 1/3 of the tomato sauce over it, and top with small dollops of ricotta and pesto, using 1/3 of each. Layer on 1/3 of the tomato slices and sprinkle with 1/3 of the mozzarella. Add another double layer of zucchini and repeat layering process twice more with the tomato sauce, pesto, ricotta and tomato slices, ending with mozzarella on top. Bake for 45-50 minutes.

Tomato Sauce

1/4 small onion, chopped
2 tbs. extra-virgin olive oil
2 16-oz. cans crushed tomatoes
1 tsp. dried oregano
1 tsp. salt
Freshly ground black pepper to taste
Pinch red-pepper flakes

In a medium saucepan or skillet, sauté onion in olive oil until translucent. Add crushed tomatoes, oregano, salt, black pepper and red-pepper flakes and simmer until flavors meld, just a few minutes.

Walnut-Basil Pesto

1/4 cup walnuts
3 cloves garlic, peeled
2 1/2 cups fresh basil leaves, packed
1/2 tsp. kosher salt
1/2 tsp. freshly ground pepper
1/2 cup good olive oil
1 cup freshly grated Parmesan

Place all ingredients in blender or food processor and blend until smooth.

Roasted Tomatoes

Oil for greasing pan
4 medium green-zebra tomatoes (or other heirloom variety)
Kosher salt

Heat oven to 250 degrees. Lightly oil baking pan or line bottom of pan with Silpat or parchment paper. Slice tomatoes 1/4-inch thick and place, in one layer, on baking pan. Sprinkle lightly with kosher salt. Roast until tomatoes have lost most of their moisture, about 1 hour.

Restoration: Neutra

When Stacey and Jeff Mann purchased this historic Richard Neutra-designed home in South Pasadena (the Wilkins House, 1949), the kitchen had been altered – some original cabinetry had been removed, and a china hutch had been screwed into the Formica countertop. When they pulled it all out to refurbish the metal cabinets, they realized that somewhere along the line, an owner had replaced the original cabinets (the handles were different). So they decided to bring it back to Neutra's original plan. There were some architectural clues: They could see some of the original framing and what the placement of the cabinets should have been. They built what they didn't have and refurbished what they could. And they added one new-era improvement: four under-counter refrigerator drawers, which Stacey loves for their convenience. This allowed them to put the Sub-Zero in the pantry, where Neutra intended the refrigerator to be.

Stacey Mann's Roast Chicken

"I clean the chicken and shove rosemary and garlic between the breast meat and the skin. I rub the whole thing down with salt and pepper, and stuff the breast cavity with lemon, apple, onion and garlic. Then I find whatever vegetables I have: potatoes, garlic, carrots, squash, maybe even beets. I toss in a little white wine and butter… we call the stuff around the chicken 'the goo.' I roast the chicken at 350 degrees, basting it all along, and when it is done, I take it out and keep roasting the veggies until they are crispy and delicious. Everybody just loves it."

From Garden to Kitchen

Attorney Michael Williamson is a double threat in the culinary arena. He grew up in England, where his mom was a terrific cook and his dad gardened; today, he loves to do both, preparing glorious meals that often begin with a visit to the vegetable beds in his San Pasqual yard. *"We have this terrific backyard,"* he says, *"with all the space needed to grow fruit trees and tomatoes and herbs."* During the week, Michael uses his drive home from downtown to think about what he'd like to make for dinner for his wife, Eileen, and himself; their sons, Sam, Nick and Jack, already will have eaten by the time he gets home. *"It is usually something relatively simple and quick on weekdays,"* he says.

The boys are all interested in what goes on in the kitchen. On weekend mornings, Jack, 3, is an official batter stirrer with his dad; big brother Sam, 13, chops, stirs and generally helps out. *"It is kind of neat, because it reminds me of what I did. But I did it in a much smaller house,"* says Michael. *"Hopefully our kids will grow their own gardens one day."* Other than weekend trips to In-N-Out, the Williamsons don't eat much takeout. *"I feel that preparing a meal that is delicious and healthy and doesn't come out of a can or a takeout container is really great for the kids."*

The Williamsons rebuilt the entire rear of their Wallace Neff house, which had a long, low, dark kitchen that was the result of a '70s remodel. They wanted a big kitchen/great room/breakfast area, so they hired an architect to get going. Ultimately, they tossed those plans and did it themselves, with Eileen acting as general contractor. The result: gorgeous! They particularly love the huge island with lots of space for cooking and homework, the old-fashioned and eminently practical butler's pantry, the capacious kitchen table, and the giant stove, a dual-fuel 60-inch Wolf with four burners, a grill, two full-size ovens and a French top (a smooth surface with different heat zones). And Michael uses it all.

Pretty much every meal that Michael prepares has wine in it in some form or another, so it should come as no surprise that he built a little winery behind the guesthouse. With a few other winemaking guys, Michael buys grapes from Napa Valley and crushes, presses and bottles the wine at home. In a peak production year, he's made about nine barrels. *"We had an absolutely fabulous pinot,"* he says, *"and we had a cabernet in 1997 with grapes from Steiner Vineyard that was terrific."*

Michael Williamson's Fresh Tomato Sauce

"Go to the garden and pick a couple of pounds of tomatoes (Michael typically has nine varieties) and give them a rough chop. Smash a couple of cloves of garlic and throw them into a deep pan with a splash of olive oil and some black pepper. Let the garlic go to a light brown, toss in the tomatoes and let the mixture reduce. Pour in some white wine and a big handful of whatever fresh herb you have on hand: mint or basil or parsley or chives."

Two Cooks in a Compact Kitchen

Jeremy Cowin and Dana Hursey live in Altadena in a small Gregory Ain Park Planned Home built in 1946. Ain, a 1949 Guggenheim grant winner, is most famous for his midcentury focus on affordable postwar housing. The house needed work, especially the kitchen, so Jeremy and Dana embarked on a remodel, aiming to open up what was a closed-off space. *"Where the curved bar is now, there was a refrigerator and a built-in pantry that went up to the ceiling, "* says Jeremy, *"We took that out to create an open space, so whoever was in the kitchen could participate in the conversation in the dining and living rooms."* They also maximized storage (wisely building an appliance garage) and counter space to make a wonderfully efficient working kitchen that can accommodate Jeremy cooking and Dana baking at the same time.

Dana's Apple Pie

8 cups (3 lbs.) Granny Smith apples, peeled and sliced
2/3 cup sugar
2/3 cup brown sugar
1 tbs. cinnamon
1/4 tsp. salt
1/2 tsp. clove
1/2 tsp. nutmeg
1 tbs. fresh lemon juice
1 tbs. lemon zest
4 tbs. butter

Place apples in large pot, and add all remaining ingredients. Simmer, covered, for a few hours (give or take). Place in unbaked crust and cover with topping (see recipe below). Bake at 350 degrees for 50-60 minutes.

Topping

1/2 cup brown sugar
1/2 cup flour
1/2 tsp. cinnamon
1/4 tsp. ginger
1/8 tsp. mace
1/4 cup melted butter

Combine in bowl until crumbly.

Everybody in the Kitchen!

While the big table in the kitchen is where the Davich family – Carrie, Marty and children Jacob, 16, Hannah, 14, and Laura, 10 – gather almost every night for dinner, the beautiful dining room is no stranger to wonderful meals. All the kids like to cook, and Hannah is particularly at home in the kitchen. *"She'll just go into the kitchen and make muffins or cupcakes,"* says Carrie. *"She's always making crepes for people and likes to help in the kitchen.*

"Food and cooking are really important to us. We have a great tradition for the past few years where my mother and my sister and her family come for Mother's Day, and my husband and son do all the cooking."

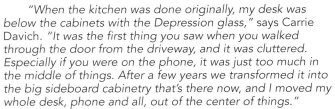

"When the kitchen was done originally, my desk was below the cabinets with the Depression glass," says Carrie Davich. *"It was the first thing you saw when you walked through the door from the driveway, and it was cluttered. Especially if you were on the phone, it was just too much in the middle of things. After a few years we transformed it into the big sideboard cabinetry that's there now, and I moved my whole desk, phone and all, out of the center of things."*

The Cabinet Kitchen

Many a glorious piece of furniture has found its way from antiques dealer Susanne Hollis to homes in Pasadena, but perhaps only one has provided the inspiration to create a black kitchen. Artist Sally Storch, whose family lives in a traditional Madison Heights colonial, calls the cabinet a final resting place for many of her favorite things. *"I bought this cabinet and started to think about building something around it,"* she says.

The room in need of remodeling was the kitchen, so Sally decided to design it around this black, turn-of-the-century cabinet from British-occupied Ceylon (today's Sri Lanka). *"It had such energy and history, and we just thought it would work,"* she says. And work they did, without a net – no architect or plans, only the cabinet as inspiration. Budgetary considerations required that they *"inch along,"* and Sally says the fact that it took so much time probably kept them from making mistakes in the design. It took an enormous effort, a long time and stubborn resolve in the face of doubting Thomases – or more accurately, doubting moms: *"My mother kept saying things like, 'What are you thinking, honey?' It felt a little risky… I knew the black would work at Christmas, but what would it be like in August?"*

Fortunately, the family loves it. In summer, they open the doors and windows and the scent of roses hovers in the room. *"We love it, we really do,"* says Sally. *"We've never looked back."* As for cooking? *"Think of the aroma of the best carne asada tacos you could ever have (a specialty of Sally's husband, painter Ray Turner), and that is this kitchen. Meals, laundry, homework… we live around this kitchen table."*

The tin ceiling (above right) was salvaged from Bethlehem Steel in Pennsylvania. Sally painted it white, a look easterners know from the many late-nineteenth- and early-twentieth-century buildings whose tin ceilings were painted white to evoke the costlier carved plasterwork popular at the time.

Right: The large antique black wall cabinet inspired Sally and her family to create a black kitchen; their dining room reflects the classic lines of their colonial revival home.

A Tall Order

When six-foot-three Bruce Ryan and his wife, five-foot-nine Loren Tripp, took on the always-challenging job of a kitchen remodel, they considered their own heights, to say nothing of the escalating heights of sons Peter – already in size ten-and-a-half shoes at age 12 – and Quincy, 8. They were inspired by the work of British kitchen designer Johnny Grey, who, says Loren, eschews the American standard of *"everything has to be from 18 to 32 inches from here to there"* in favor of a more organic approach that uses different heights for different tasks.

While doing the remodel, the family lived in an apartment over the garage, where the cramped quarters and low sink with cabinet above meant that, says Loren, *"To do the dishes, we'd have to step back, lean forward and rest our heads against the cabinet."* As one might imagine, this learning by experience helped the couple refine their design to prevent future backaches. The original four-room area – galley kitchen, maid's bedroom and bath and utility porch – in their 1913 Altadena home became one large, sunny room with varied heights for countertops and sink to best suit the work areas.

The Backyard Gourmet

We asked psychotherapist and mother of two Chris Jansen-Gillum to name something quick and easy that her family enjoys eating, and the answer came immediately from her 17-year-old daughter, Darah: goat cheese salad. Darah's friends love it, too. On a summer evening, the South Pasadena backyard table is prepped, and everyone fills a plate and steps outside to eat. *"It's cooler outside; the birds are singing and the breeze is blowing,"* says Chris. *"We're under a big tree and looking at one another, and it is perfect."*

Darah and her friends are fans of her mom's cooking, so Chris and the kids cook some of their favorite dishes together, and she's turning their work into a recipe book for each to carry off to college.

Goat Cheese Salad

Toss together a bag or two of salad greens (depending on how many are eating), fresh basil and dill, crumbled goat cheese, thinly sliced red pepper and red onion, chopped almonds, a handful of chopped cranberries, olive oil, balsamic vinegar, salt and pepper.

Left: Chris Jansen-Gillum feeds the teens in her South Pasadena backyard.

Above, clockwise from upper left: the butler's pantry in the Whitfords' Wallace Neff home; a clean-lined corner of the Whitford kitchen; the serpentine lines of the Whitfords' butler's pantry sink; the Williamsons' duel-fuel 60-inch Wolf range; Georgina Whitford's teapots.

It's All in the Details

It takes a moment to recognize the cleverness of a subtle design element in the small, efficient kitchen of this ultimate loft in Pasadena's historic Castle Green: Beneath the windows, four drawers are flush with an outside wall, with no counter above them to indicate any depth. The secret? They are built out beyond the wall into the large outdoor terrace. *"Whoever thought of it is really brilliant,"* says Matthew White, who was named one of *Architectural Digest*'s 100 top designers in the world and is co-owner (with Frank Webb) of White Webb, a Manhattan design firm.

"It was done before we arrived," says Matthew of the disappearing drawers. *"But we do a lot of entertaining, so we clad the box that surrounds the exterior drawer space in copper. That protects it from the elements and makes a beautiful surface for serving. The kitchen windows open inward, and you can actually set food up on this copper buffet space by passing it right through the window."*

White and his partner, theatrical producer Thomas Schumacher, now live in New York, but while in Pasadena they did an extensive renovation of the loft and enjoyed the space immensely. They added a capacious outdoor barbecue that extended the kitchen's facility for preparing large meals, from fundraising dinners for 60 on the terrace to sit-down dinners for twelve at the large glass table (whose day job is to serve as Matthew's desk).

Clockwise from above: The terrace outside Matthew White and Thomas Schumacher's Castle Green penthouse; the built-out kitchen drawers sit under a window that's used to pass food out to the terrace; Matthew White's glass-topped table, dressed for its day job.

Let's Table This for Now...

Margaret and David and their two daughters, Kathryn, 17, and Madlyn, 16, have a big family and a lot of friends. They love to entertain, they do a lot of it, and they do not throw the same party every time. *"We needed versatility, and we are so happy with the way this house provides it,"* says Margaret. *"It may be a family gathering, a corporate dinner or friends from out of town – and sometimes all in the same few days!"*

To make the parties possible, they have an outdoor dining table and grill, as well as four tables central to the dining and kitchen areas that can graciously accommodate both large and intimate gatherings. The blond kitchen table is ideal for family breakfasts and dinners; the round pedestal table works well for mature family members who find a couch challenging to rise from; and the two custom-made dining room tables can comfortably seat eighteen when the occasion arises – and it does. The black, five-foot-square tables stay in place (under lighting designed for them), and a section is added between them (illuminated by recessed lighting). *"We have a large extended family, and I wanted us to be able to sit down comfortably to a meal together,"* says Margaret. *"But I did not want to sit at a massive, long table when we were only four."*

Margaret is a great cook with a great kitchen, and that is no happy accident. She was already thinking about her dream kitchen when they closed escrow on the property on which they were to build their home. She went to all the manufacturers' demonstration classes: Dacor, Viking and Thermador twice, each about a year apart, so she could stay current on new products. This serious home chef, who is not fazed by feeding a small (if friendly) army, considered every element of design, decor, cleanup and capacity. She knew she wanted additional wall ovens, so the ultimate criterion for choosing her main range and oven was simple: which will accommodate a 23-pound turkey with room to spare? She decided on the Thermador six-burner range with one huge oven, which she uses when cooking for a large gathering.

What's for Dinner at Margaret and David's?

Caterers love Margaret's kitchen, but she is also an accomplished cook and baker. On a recent weekend, the caterers were in for a party of 90, but the next night, Margaret cooked for her family and two friends from out of town, and David pulled some wine from his cellar. The trick is to keep it simple.

Hors d'oeuvres

Hummus and a roasted red pepper tapenade with walnuts and pomegranates, served with crudités and pita chips.

Dinner

Fresh halibut with chili-lime butter and rice pilaf

1. Ahead of time, prep fresh halibut with olive oil and salt and place on baking tray, which goes into the fridge.
2. Make some rice pilaf.
3. Remove halibut from fridge a few minutes before baking, add a bit of wine to baking tray before popping into 400-degree oven for 12 minutes. Cover with chili-lime butter.

Serve with a 2005 Hippolyte Reverdy Sancerre wine.

Dessert

Flourless chocolate cake from Whole Foods, topped with fresh berries and Häagen-Dazs vanilla ice cream.

Gardening:
at home

What do we want from our gardens? Many of the same things we want from our homes: shelter, privacy and a place to gather, play, unwind. Modern-day gardens are the scions of that which our forebears developed 5,000 years ago, when agriculture was created in the Fertile Crescent by nomads no more, the Mesopotamians, from the Greater Mesopotamian cradle, and Ancient Egyptians. These highly skilled civilizations, the first to develop written language, also developed irrigation for stretches of dry land beyond the alluvium, or river-washed soils of the Tigris and Euphrates, and the Nile and Jordan. Naturally fertilized lands and the desert climate created perfect conditions for seed-bearing annuals, especially grains. In surplus, these foodstuffs sustained the development of the population. Sustenance aside, some of those early farming objectives translate to our contemporary gardens. We still want food, medicinal relief, a sense of order and accomplishment, a chance to experiment, and the pleasure of being surrounded by beauty and fragrance. We want predictability and surprise, and not just in the form of the monthly water bill. We want a reflection of the world we inhabit, a reminder of another time, and the wonder of what we can plan and accomplish in an afternoon, a weekend, a lifetime.

To plant the grounds of a manor house, or to tend a humble strip in the side yard, we start with climate and soil. Latitude, ocean, valleys and mountains define the San Gabriel Valley's weather. At the base of the east-west running, or transverse, San Gabriel Mountains, and southeast of the Santa Monica Mountains, Pasadena is located in one of the world's five Mediterranean zones. Cold spots and thermal belts are tempered by maritime air. Mild, wet winters and hot, dry summers are dogged by the Santa Ana winds in late fall. Their speed and low humidity clear smoggy skies and cook plants. Visitors routinely comment on our crystal skies, while locals are just plain annoyed, temporarily living in a staticky, skin-crisping town where their cars are never clean.

Pasadena's soil began as thousands of years of mountain runoff of clay, gravel, silt and sand, combined with arboreal litter. The rich soil that slid into our valley became money in the banco, first for the Original Peoples who hunted and gathered here, then for the 18th-century Spanish mission settlers, and finally for the citizens of the new American state of California. Although native plant gardens have gained favor in recent years, some of Pasadena's most widely cultivated plants remain citrus and roses, both of which were introduced by the Spanish.

As a whole, gardeners in and around Pasadena are a generous lot. They tend to work more and talk less, and they won't always tell you how many hours they spend in the garden each week. Gardening is a year-round job here, so watching the clock doesn't really help much anyway. But ask a gardener, and she or he will share enthusiasm, sources and, yes, the bumper crop of dreaded zucchini. Our weekend warriors are hardy, capable types who enjoy most tasks involved in caring for lawns, flower beds and vegetable plots. When landscaping machines arrived in the 1920s, old-school full-time gardeners were pruned away, making room for subdivisions, smaller plots and the necessity of doing it yourself or hiring today's

mow-blow-and-go professionals. So if a person doesn't want to weed and cultivate the soil, no problem. Someone else can tidy things up for a modest sum.

Unless you are a kid whose mom locked you outside until you filled up that bucket with weeds, chances are that when you're in the garden, there's nowhere else you want to be. Because mulching, weeding, hand watering, dividing and constructing compost bins long past sunset brings sore muscles and great rewards.

– SG

Garden books popular among many Pasadena-area gardeners:

American Horticultural Society A to Z Encyclopedia of Garden Plants, H. Marc Cathey
Desert Gardens, Gary Lyons
The Education of a Gardener, Russell Page
The Gardens of California, Nancy Goslee Power
Index of Garden Plants: The New Royal Horticultural Society Dictionary, Mark Griffiths
Sun Drenched Gardens: The Mediterranean Garden, Jan Smithen
Western Garden Book, *Sunset* magazine editors
The Year I Ate My Garden, Tony Kienitz

They also get involved in one or many of the following organizations, which combine education, preservation and community service:

Arlington Garden
The California Succulent Society
Descanso Bonsai Society
Descanso Gardens
Eaton Canyon
The Garden Conservancy
The Huntington Botanical Gardens
International Geranium Club, Los Angeles branch
L.A. County Arboretum
The Mediterranean Garden Society
Pasadena Beautiful
Theodore Payne Foundation
Rancho Santa Ana Botanic Garden
Southern California Camellia Societies
Southern California Horticultural Society

Left page: Elaine Carhartt and John Reveley use as many recycled materials as possible in their garden; they made this cold case out of old wood and a repurposed French door.

Right page, clockwise from upper left: Even hose storage is handled creatively in the Reveley/Carhartt garden; the Reveley/Carhartt chicken coop; a pocket vineyard in Ann Cutting and Tom Soulanille's southwest Pasadena yard; Louisa Miller's basket of homegrown lavender; the tools of Louisa Miller's trade; John Reveley's vintage Ford is part of the gardenscape.

The Yariv Gardens: Mediterranean on the Arroyo

In the Yariv gardens, Italian Renaissance meets the Moors.

Some of the most graceful California gardens draw on the state's mixed horticultural heritage. The intertwining of history, plants and aesthetics is amplified in Fran and Amnon Yariv's garden, which was designed by their daughter, landscape architect Gabriela Yariv. The massive gray-green agaves that line the street like giant thorny bouncers at a nightclub you're not cool enough to get into invite expectation from the parkway outside.

The drive is framed by a vine-covered garage and stairs that lead to the house, a Mediterranean-style villa on the edge of the Arroyo. A dry fountain bowl, wall mounted, has tiny succulents popping over its lip, a whimsical twist on a water feature. Pathways and stairs lead past a great lawn with a comma of round, sculpted hedges, echoing the ripple of waves. Even before we find the pool, we encounter another reference to the curative powers of water and a tranquil garden: a stand of 30-foot-tall cypress trees shooting up from the lawn, like water amusements from a 16th-century Italian garden. The quatrefoil swimming pool, Moorish in influence, is discreetly tucked into an upper corner, framed by a rounded wrought-iron gate.

Near the pool is a small citrus grove, heavy with lemons and blossoms, and a bed of roses that looks like it was just heaved up by the earth as an offering. In the back, the villa is enclosed by cozy patios, nooks and an open-air dining room, its thick drapes tied back, waiting to defend against the sun. A well draws the eye back toward the northeast corner, past an urn-shaped pot, a pocket of ferns, a vine-covered arbor, a path and potted evergreens. In the calm of midday, this multileveled retreat makes paradise seem possible.

61

The Folly Bowl
Susanna Dadd & James Griffith

Susanna Dadd and James Griffith collaborated on the design and construction of the Folly Bowl, a concrete amphitheater on the western flank of their hillside property. Their midcentury home rests next to a small, rocky canyon in the Altadena foothills. At the Folly Bowl, the play's the thing – or the string-ensemble recital or the poetry reading. Over an eight-year period, the Dadd-Griffiths have reshaped their half-acre by hand. They added rocks and boulders, moved earth, dug in truckloads of locally made mulch, reinforced the slopes and planted new native flora. On the eastern half of their land, they created an oak woodland.

As in much of Pasadena, the Dadd-Griffiths live within several microclimates, sometimes a few feet from one another. Rivers of cold air course next to warmer hillsides. Sunny spots can be harsh in winter or summer. One solution: growing shade trees and part-shade scrubs to buffer the environment.

Susanna was given her first garden plot at the age of 4, which she promptly filled with toadstools from the nearby woods. Evolving as an artist and a gardener, she follows her father, who was a serious English plantsman. He created a scholar's botanical garden, Ballalheannagh, on the Isle of Man. The Dadd-Griffith's California native garden is quite different from her father's 40-acre undertaking, but the two share similar topography. Both use clever pathways to access steep hillsides, and both are carefully anchored with local rock and native plant combinations. *"I learned from my father that anything is possible once you determine what it is that you want,"* she says. James continues to plant vegetables, as he did as a teenager, once determined to be a self-sufficient farmer. Now at the Folly Bowl, he shares tomatoes with foraging deer.

1916 Japanese Garden
Karen & Ed Miller

This old Japanese garden was originally built in 1916 as one of several themed garden "rooms" in the terraced landscape of an estate belonging to Thomasella Graham. In 1913 Graham entreated Tokataro Kato, a Japanese priest from the Imperial Court, to travel to Sierra Madre to build her an authentic meditation garden. The story goes that Kato sat silently on the property for nine months, studying the land before moving a single stone.

The traditional design forces of rock placement, representing heaven (vertical), earth (horizontal) and man (diagonal lines), figure prominently. And just as ancient garden-building techniques passed from China to Korea to Japan, the use of local materials emerged, clearing the path for the use of California trees here in Sierra Madre. Even though the original sloped property was subdivided and sold off by 1949, the garden still has a view that extends several miles south.

The Millers spend time in the garden every day. From the big picture windows inside the house, the life of the garden isn't forsaken, even on chilly winter days. The light moves through the leaves and branches in patterns with the seasons. Birds populate the trees and stream. The carp multiply in spring, keeping the ponds clean by feeding on algae. Ground covers are pruned regularly to prevent domination. Special occasions, such as birthday parties and *Little House on the Prairie* play dates for the Millers' daughter, enliven the teahouse. Karen sweeps and rakes the pathways and admires the garden's constant, natural state of degradation. *"If this place isn't allowed to age, what is?"* Karen asks, segueing into a discussion of *wabi-sabi*, the Japanese art of finding beauty in imperfection, in appreciating the natural cycle of growth, decay and death. A thriving bamboo stand in front and an antique carved-wood gate are the quiet clues that some things precious are harbored here. This iconic garden. That playful dog. This singing, dancing, cartwheel-turning 8-year-old. Together they converge, restful yet invigorated, in an old Japanese garden.

Suburban Woods
Louisa Miller

Louisa Miller, her husband, Bob, and their children moved into their Pasadena home in the 1970s. The house was electric yellow and in need of attention. Over the years, in addition to overseeing a phased remodel, Louisa turned the soil and planted perennials, large shrubs and trees: sixteen in the back, eleven in the front. Louisa did the heavy lifting, but the garden had to work for the whole family – even Bob, whose allergies to a mature mulberry tree kept him indoors for three weeks each year. Says Louisa, *"He was miserable. Well, that was no good. So I took the tree out."* Nobody ever said Louisa is not direct.

What stayed: liquidambar for shade, Japanese maples for color, redbud and Chinese fringe, dwarf Golden Dorset, Anna and Fuji apples, a plum tree and two figs, which her daughter propagated from a family tree in Texas. Louisa's backyard erupts with mixed perennial beds bordered by mature camellias and yellow Lady Banks roses, which bloom with the lavender wisteria vines that are cut back hard every other year.

Louisa has been gardening since smoking was fashionable. She has taken horticulture classes at Rancho Santa Ana Botanic Gardens, attended lectures and workshops with various garden groups, divided hundreds of irises and built hundreds of container gardens for civic projects. She has a great eye for color and composition, foundation plants and surprises. And she has a recurring conversation with her gardener, who piles grass clippings around her tree trunks: *"All these years, and I still can't get him to compost. He just doesn't believe in it!"* She laughs, not quite exasperated, and moves on, pulling a weed here and there as she goes.

An Artist's Eye
Marcia & Ed Nunnery

Fine artists with backgrounds in ceramic and metal sculpture, filmmaking and painting, the Nunnerys own Aarnun Gallery & Fine Picture Framing in Pasadena.

Says Marcia: *"What did we want from this garden? Well, the house was built in 1958. When we bought it, we wanted to revert to the original intent. We removed brick and white paint, the brass lanterns outside the door… all the colonial treatment. The house is built into a hillside, in a cascading setting. We wanted to magnify that. For art, you think, Whose work do you like? And for landscaping – which is an art you live with every day – you ask, Who do you like to work with? Then, what structure is needed? We needed hardscape to reinforce the house built into the hill, and to balance the big stone pines on the property. And we had an ash tree that was not a gorgeous specimen, but we loved it. We wanted to enjoy the dappled light it gave. We have a particular view from our canyon of oak and eucalyptus in the distance. We wanted to see them. And we wanted privacy.*

"We're out here in the garden every day. I'll say, 'I'm going on a tour. Do you want to come?' Or some days, if I seem like I need some quiet time – Ed's good about sensing that – he'll ask, 'Is it okay if I come?' So, we tour. We stand in one spot and watch the breeze or birds in the trees. I water or weed on the tour. We sit in different places to see what's new."

The Nunnerys' hillside is reinforced by a poured-concrete retaining wall. Because of the slope, such ground covers as creeping thyme, carpet bugle, penstemon and prostrate rosemary offer fire resistance and prevent soil erosion. Landscape architect Rick Button called out specific concrete pedestals for Ed's metal dog sculptures, which serve as sentries on the patio. Elemental earth and water meet in the mix as sea shells were pressed into the concrete just before drying, imitating evolutionary strata. The custom iron screen, a takeoff on an urban scape in one of Ed's paintings, gives privacy from a neighboring house, while a pair of local crows visit the Mayan fountain daily for drinks and water play.

Ramps & Paths

Gwen Babcock

Gwen Babcock and her husband, Gil, have lived in this San Marino neighborhood for forty years and in this house for ten. They designed the garden to work for Gwen's wheelchair. Raised beds anchor the vegetable garden for winter and summer crops. With numerous brick and concrete ramps, Gwen easily traverses the circular path around their hilltop retreat.

A canopy of treetops in Lacy Park below is the central view from the Babcocks' garden. Gwen's favorite spot is on the deck under the old coast live oak. It's cool and serene here most of the year, except during the park's 4th of July celebration, when the Babcocks' family and friends gather on the lawn, watching the stars give way to fireworks.

A Talk with Landscape Architect
Heather Lenkin

Many of the gardens featured on these pages are lovingly tended by the homeowner's hand, and they are not alone. Gardening is the most popular do-it-yourself hobby in the United States, with some 83 percent of the adult population maintaining lawns, flowers or vegetables. What do we plant? Fruits and nuts in California, as the old joke goes. Actually, it's fruits and vegetables. Homegrown edibles are slightly more represented than ornamental flower gardens. So adults have learned not only to eat their vegetables but to grow them, too.

No matter how grand or minute the project, many home gardeners consult a professional. Where they might cautiously take a year in a new home to watch the patterns of the sun and gauge soil drainage before planting a daisy (and there's not a thing wrong with that approach), a landscape architect can expedite the process. Even if hiring one is not in the budget, you can learn from them at hands-on classes through botanical venues and county programs (see Resource Guide).

Some of the most lush and inspired designs in Pasadena belong to landscape architect Heather Lenkin, A.I.A., ASLA. Her private, one-acre garden is divided into twenty-one themed "rooms," featuring terraces, mazes, a potting/lathe house, a succulent garden, hundreds of roses and more than 12,000 bulbs. She has studied in the American southwest, Italy and France, and her early works were influenced by Frank

Lloyd Wright's Prairie school of architecture in her native Illinois. Heather's Southern California commissions have been featured in *Fine Gardening, Garden Design, Cottage Living* and *Woman's Day,* she is a repeat recipient of the Golden Trowel Award for excellence in landscape design, and her own garden was selected by *Fine Gardening* as one of the ten "Great Gardens" of the United States. It has been a tour destination on behalf of the Pasadena Museum of History, the Garden Conservancy, the Mediterranean Garden Society, the Northwest Horticultural Society and the San Marino League, among others. One of her recent projects involved designing a four-season wedding garden pavilion, on permanent display at the L.A. County Arboretum, built around a replica of the gazebo that Luke and Laura, from *General Hospital,* were married in.

Sandy asked Heather Lenkin to sit in a shady spot to answer a few questions.

Q: What are the main considerations when planning a garden?

A: There are quite a few. First, consider the big picture, which, to start with, is geographic. Where's the site? What's the orientation? North- or west-facing? Is it sunny, shady, hilly, steep? Then we want to determine what plant materials work well for the site. So we see what's already growing. Other considerations include the tree canopy, and determining what the native pests are. Deer? Gophers? Natural considerations?

Q: How long does it take you to assess a garden site?

A: That depends on the size of the property, of course. But a half-acre residential lot should take, oh, about two hours to map. The thing is, a lot of people really enjoy doing this themselves, which is great. If you don't want to do this yourself, you can hire someone. The simplest plan can be a reasonable representation of the dimensions and a plant list. Include any existing bulbs that will come up next spring and an inventory of trees. That idea of not touching a garden at your new house for a year isn't a bad idea. I know someone who once took out a mature tree that was dead. Turns out it was deciduous, and was simply dormant. They lost a gorgeous specimen because they didn't know what the garden would provide.

Q: Is it okay to copy someone else's garden?

A: That's a bit tricky. It's absolutely great to be inspired by what you see. But don't jump in and copy before you make sure those plans fit your site.

Q: So don't plant a shade garden in a sunny field?

A: There you go. Even if you have plenty of shade for that garden, you must take the time to make sure your drainage is adequate, and that your soil can provide for those plants. If you want a drought-tolerant garden or a cottage garden or a water-loving garden, you must provide for a complete marriage between soil and irrigation. If you can't do that, you should reassess.

Q: Is there such thing as a Pasadena garden?

A: Hmm, well, as in much of Southern California, there is a huge variety in microclimates and architecture here in Pasadena. Which means there's a great diversity of garden styles, and many could work at most houses. The thing is, different people use gardens in different ways. This goes back to the big considerations. I poll the family… how will they use the garden? What are the ages of the children? Do they like to eat dinner outside? Do they want privacy around the pool? Will they be weeding the beds themselves? Do they want to do that on their knees or would they rather not bend that far? For my cottage garden, I made the bed width the same as the length of my arm, because that's how far I can reach. I'm out there to have fun, not to get injured!

Q: How do you use your garden?

A: Professionally, I use it for experimenting botanically, trying new materials. I want to be able to recommend newly introduced plants, so I note their properties. I collect seeds and cuttings. I propagate. Sometimes I just sit and admire the fragrance. I love being in the garden. I love the colors, the scents, I enjoy seeing it change and unfold. It challenges me. Plants make me laugh sometimes. Did you see my house leek? I thought that was the funniest thing, and I couldn't resist them. I installed a lot of house leeks… where else would you have a house leak? On the roof. Okay, apparently break time is over.

73

Gardening for the Common Good:
The Pasadena Garden Club & the Diggers

Garden clubs developed as educational and social venues in the 19th century, at the same time as Industrial Age scientific methods brought huge improvements to the quality of life. New were tin cans for preserving foods, machinery to crush bones for fertilizer, mass production of wire fencing, the steel plow and leisure time, with information-rich books and magazines to read during that leisure time. In 1804 our British cousins established the elite Royal Horticultural Society, right around the time that three quarters of the United States population were hoeing out their own meals. Third President and First Plantsman Thomas Jefferson loved his farmlands. *"No occupation is so delightful to me as the culture of the earth,"* he said, *"and no culture comparable to that of the garden."* He encouraged appreciation of the "poisonous" *tomatas*, planted sour oranges and olives, and loved his fig trees, considered a vulgar fruit. (To be given "the fig" – two fingers and thumb thrust toward one's mouth, like a TV chef making the sign for delicious – was a great insult.)

When green thumbs need a bit of guidance, they can consult bonsai, camellia, rose, ikebana, orchid, fuchsia, geranium, iris, desert garden and succulent societies, all found in the Pasadena area. The California Native Plant Society, the California Mediterranean Plant Society, the Arroyo Seco Foundation, the Garden Conservancy, the Creative Arts Group, the California Oak Foundation, the Theodore Payne Foundation, the Rancho Santa Ana Botanic Garden, the L.A. County Arboretum, the Huntington Botanical Gardens and Descanso Gardens all have educational components; many offer plant or seed exchanges, welcome volunteers and have civic missions. And all are good places to learn to become a better gardener at home.

But we are here to draw attention to two particularly meritorious garden groups in the Pasadena area, whose members leave their home gardens to labor for the common good. The Pasadena Garden Club was formed in 1916 so like-minded amateur horticulturalists could share the love of gardening. Myron Hunt and Theodore Payne were original card-carriers; today, all of the 100-plus group are women, and if you'd like to join, well, don't hold your breath. The roster has been full for years, because nobody ever quits, and it's rumored that a handful of sustaining members clearly remember Truman's inauguration. This is a passionate group whose dedication has maintained the grounds of local schools, museums and city streets when other resources were lacking. PGC historically has made conservation a priority, participating in education and action programs under the umbrella of the Garden Club of America. It created a foundation for the maintenance of La Casita del Arroyo, the 1933 WPA project on the lip of the lower Arroyo. This charming Myron Hunt "little house" is owned by the city of Pasadena and was originally built with local stone and wood reclaimed from the Rose Bowl bicycle track from the 1932 Olympics. PGC recently sponsored water-wise landscaping designed by Isabelle Greene; earlier campaigns included the 1927 beautification of Mt. Wilson and a 1942 war effort. The group also has catalogued more than 50 notable private Pasadena gardens for the GCA's collection in the Archives of American Gardens at the Smithsonian Institution. Many of these gardens were recorded originally on hand-painted glass slides, now part of the Smithsonian's archives.

The smaller Diggers was formed in 1924 by seven women who enjoyed doing their own gardening – but they were careful in wording their bylaws, because an incumbent president had eight gardeners tending her estate. So the original rules carefully stated that a member must have a garden "to which she gives her personal attention," a wink to Madame President and a nod to Thomas Jefferson. Diggers, more than 60 of them today, still give their personal attention to their own gardens, as well as sit on the board at the L.A. County Arboretum, steer the Descanso Bonsai Society and stay involved with the Garden Conservancy. And none of these gardeners are vacating their seats, either, so don't even think about it. The Diggers annual fundraiser is a quiet riot, sort of *A Night at the Opera* with the Diggers themselves playing both Margaret Dumont and the Marx Brothers. Conservation, preservation of native flora and a love of plants stand shoulder to shoulder with working hard while having fun. Their plant sale is one of the hottest tickets each spring, and their potted containers have a national reputation. All proceeds from the annual fundraiser support the exterior maintenance at El Molino Viejo on Old Mill Road in San Marino, and their dues cover membership in the Garden Club of America, which provides education and through which civic projects have become priorities, including flower-bed maintenance at the old Pasadena Hospital and installations on South Lake Avenue.

El Molino Viejo

Heather Lenkin's List of Long-Blooming Perennials (Minimum bloom: 6 to 10 weeks)

Agastache species
Allium senescens 'Blue Twister'
Anthemis tinctoria 'Susanna Mitchell' Marguerite daisy
Antirrhinum Snapdragon
Aquilegia chrysantha, desertorum 'Swallowtail' Columbine
Asclepias tuberosa Butterfly Weed
Aster frikarti 'Monch'
Bellium minutum Mat Daisy
Berlandiera lyrata Chocolate Daisy
Buddleia varieties Butterfly Bush
Callirhoe species Poppy Mallow
Calylophus Sundrops
Campanula rotundifolia Bluebells
Campsis radicans, Trumpet Vine
Centaurea montana Mountain Bluet
Centranthus ruber Jupiter's Beard
Ceratostigma plumbaginaceae Plumbago
Chilopsis 'Timeless Beauty' Desert Willow
Chrysanthemum 'Snow Cap' Shasta Daisy
Coreopsis varieties Tickseed
Delosperma species Hardy iceplant
Dianthus
Diascia varieties Twinspur
Echinacea purpurea Coneflower
Echinops Globe Thistle
Fallugia paradoxa Apache Plume
Gaillardia varieties Blanket Flower
Gaura varieties Apple Blossom Grass
Gazania 'Tanager' Cold Hardy Gazania
Geranium 'Johnson's Blue' Hardy geranium
Gypsophila paniculata Baby's Breath
Helenium Helen's Flower, Sneezewood
Heliopsis 'Summer Sun' perennial sunflower
Hemerocallis Daylily
Hesperaloe parviflora Texas red yucca
Heuchera Coral Bells
Hirpicium ameriodes Grassleaf Mat Daisy
Hymenoxys acaulis Sundancer Daisy
Hypericum St. John's Wort
Knautia macedonica
Lavatera Mallow
Lavandula Lavender
Liatris Blazing Star, Gayfeather
Mirabilis multiflorus
Monarda Bee Balm
Nepeta Catmint
Oenothera Evening primrose
Origanum libanoticum Oregano
Penstemon alomosensis psudospectabilis x, superbus, pinoflius
Perovskia Russian Sage
Phlox
Physostegia Obedience plant
Potentilla
Ratibida Mexican Hat
Rosa x 'John Cabot'
Rudbeckia

Salvia Sage
Saponaria ocymoides 'Alba' Soapwort
Scrophularia macrantha Red Birds
Scutellaria Skullcap
Sedum 'Autumn Joy' Stonecrop
Solidago Goldenrod
Stachys coccinea Hedge Nettle
Stokesia Stokes' Aster
Teucrium Germander
Verbena
Veronica Speedwell
Viola corsica Perennial Pansy
Zauscheria
Zinnia species Perennial Zinnia

Heather's Favorite California Natives

Aquilegia chrysantha 'Yellow Queen'
Dudleya pulverulenta Chalk Lettuce
Echium plantagineum 'Blue Bedder'
Erysimum capitatum Western Wallflower
Hyptis emoryi Desert Lavender
Lewisia cotyledon 'Sunset Strain'
Limonium californium Coastal Statice
Linum lewisii
Mimulus cardinalis
Penstemon heterophyllus
Salvia clevelandii
Sedum spathulifolium
Sidalcea bellum
Sisyrinchium bellum

Heather's General-Purpose Soil Amendment

3 lbs. soil sulphur/100 s.f.
1-inch-thick, composted leaf mold (oak leaves are great)
1-inch-thick peat moss
1 sack/100 s.f. steer manure
5 lbs./100 s.f. bone meal
Gypsum (if clay is a problem)

Apply all ingredients at the same time, turn into the soil at least to the depth of all matter, then soak. Plant, or let rest until ready for planting.

Bathing:

at home

Watch any grainy home movies from childhood, or from our collective memory courtesy of Hollywood, Bollywood or YouTube, and you'll see happy children in a bathtub, making silly beards from bubbles and chasing rubber submarines through the clawfoot deep. Or at the seaside, walking with Mommy in her funny waist-high two-piece, building a castle with Dad and Buddy, hollering when the waves carry that treasured manor back from whence it came. The camera is rarely present to record summer days with a Water Wiggle or Slip 'n' Slide, because by that age you're old enough to play in the backyard without adult supervision, and Mom and Dad assume you won't break your neck. If you survive, you move on to cannon balls off the deep end, swim team at the Rose Bowl or the Valley Hunt Club or, better yet, a short board in Carlsbad. For your parents' sake, hopefully you're paying for your own apartment by the time you reach the fork in the road: one direction, training for triathlons; the other, skinny-dipping in hot tubs, likely the road straight to Hades (or Nirvana, but only time will tell). Somewhere in between these frolics and membership in the Polar Bear Club (meetings commence in any Pasadena swimming pool in November), there are luxurious afternoons sipping iced tea on an inflatable chair in your own pool. Equally restorative are spa soaks, splashes in the fountain, sitting in the shallow end, filling the birdbath, diving into a bathtub, and spritzing in the shower. Brushing your teeth in the tiny vintage sink you paid for with the sweat of your labors can also represent the finest of daily water rituals. Even if the Super 8's not whirring, smile and enjoy every drop.

And, yes, now it's time for the lecture about how precious water is. In its natural state, Southern California is a desert. The industrialists and developers who built Pasadena pitched the place as a land of sunshine, waterfalls and good fortune for all. Engineering and politics brought water, which we still believe is a God-given right. Our typical bath uses 35 gallons, and a ten-minute shower pours 60 gallons down the drain.

Hung out to dry are the ancient practices of the public bath, which were once vital community centers. Egyptians, Assyrians, Greeks and Romans had community baths with hot water, sand scrubs, vapors, cooling plunges and oils. In Greece and Rome, boys' elementary education included swimming lessons, and Japan of the first century BC shows records of swimming competitions. The Romans kept roaming all the way to England, building roads and walls as they marched to locations with therapeutic mineral waters, such as Aquae Sulis, which we know today as Bath, the only English hot springs. After the Romans, fears of water-born disease and infection kept the Anglos out of the dip until water therapy at the seashore became popular in the late 17th century and the famed Turkish baths were developed, using warm and hot water and steam. In part because it is precious and loaded with symbolism, water is used for ritual washings and purifications by many religions: at the confluence of two rivers, for major and minor ablutions, and for women's baths, baptisms and foot-washings.

Back home in our desert, unpredictable winter rains and climbing summer temperatures slowly drip into our

consciousness, reminding us, in case we forgot, that water is precious. Echoing through the ages, water represents life, grapes instead of raisins, time for relaxing instead of toiling, the buoyancy that's possible even when gravity is present. Don't waste it, but do enjoy it. Last one in's a rotten egg.

– SG

Clockwise from right: Gold-tiled 1960 master bathroom built by Annaly Bennett's parents has a cutting-edge-for-the-era sunken tub, dual sinks and door handles purchased from Sarah Bernhardt's estate; the powder bath at designer Carolyn Watson's 1905 Arts & Crafts Transitional home showcases restored original hardware and Japanese-influenced furnishings; this master bath features Italian blue glass tiles that remind owner Ender Sezgin of his Turkish childhood, where the color blue is said to protect against envy; the tub has a hygienic air-jet massage system that ejects all water from the previous use.

Everyone in the Tub!

The oversize bathtub in the master bathroom makes Prospect Park homeowner Carrie Davich laugh. *"It's a showpiece,"* she says. *"It's beautiful, and I credit our decorator, Michael Berman, with convincing us to put it in. But it's sort of funny that the big statement of the house is the bathtub."* The "before" picture of the master bath featured a sunken tub, flush with the floor. Light came from one small window in the exterior wall, and the square doorway from sink to tub was tiled. *"The bathroom was really dark, and it made the master bedroom dark, too,"* says Carrie. *"It's a one-story house, so we had to find a way to maximize the amount of light that could come in."*

Enter the remodel phase of the Daviches' lives. First, they popped out the big bathroom window, adding views of a garden pathway shaded by a grape-clad pergola over a stacked stone wall. The new floor-to-ceiling bowed bay window added both light and square footage. *"There are five windows in the bathroom now,"* says Carrie. *"Two on either side of the sink. And the bay. It's a dramatic difference. The bedroom is so much lighter, too."* They also created a curved archway that works well with the curves of the tub. The cool marble floor reflects light, and the steam shower has overhead spray and a hand-held diverter.

"My daughters love the big bathtub best," says Carrie. *"They thinks it's a really fun place to be."*

Clockwise from top: Original textured glass window in the Daviches' renovated master bathroom; their mirrored breakfront and heated towel rack; the dressing room boasts another original window; bowed bay windows illuminate the free-standing tub; the marble-topped double vanity carries an ebony stain; his and hers robes hang on the ready by the shower door.

Two Tickets to Paradise

Norma and Gary Cowles live in a splendid Spanish colonial revival manor house designed by Bertram Goodhue, built in 1915 and lovingly restored by the Cowleses over a three-year period. Well, there's restored and there's knock-your-socks-off, which is every inch of this 10,000-square-foot palace. Say, while your socks are off, let's head up to the master bathroom. You'll want to feel this marble-tiled floor and oversize Persian rug with your bare feet. Please, sit on the couch. The full-size couch in the bathroom. In this Moor-kissed bathroom suite, the exotic amenities go on and on. There's a fireplace and a "his" sink with a cast-limestone counter and faux base that seems to float above the floor. Above the sink is a flush-mounted mirror framed with blue patterned tile. The Cowleses imported a team of seventh-generation Moroccan artisans from Fez who spent three and a half months doing the tile work for this spa retreat. The walls and tub surround are tiled, as is the walk-in shower and steam room, which Gary uses every day. *"The dogs even walk in there sometimes and get a nice little spray,"* says Norma.

Across the room from "his" sink, Norma's vanity is a freestanding wooden cabinet with a wooden framed mirror. She has her own tub, too, which is placed across from the fireplace and capped with turned-wood vaulting. Does she use this aquatic confection often? *"Oh, yes, I love it!"* she says. *"It's a very comfortable tub, although it's a bit too big for me. I can practically swim from one end to the other."*

Like a Persian oasis, from the Cowles estate spring refreshing waters, which flow on an axis from front to back and fill three fountains. In the front court, a cherubic bronze Pan readies to play from a miniature moat inside a small pool. *"There's a rill that the water follows, down to the driveway, and recirculates."* says Norma. *"And from the reflecting pool in the back is a fountain facing the house, with another Pan facing away. Through this second Pan, the water travels a bit farther before recirculating."* Classically symmetrical, this channel bisects a series of steps ending in a blue dot, which gives the fountain a bonus: It looks like a thermometer, reminding us that it's going to be a scorcher, so why not cool off in the pool? So we look for the swimming pool, which entices with a circular fan of steps.

"We have beautiful bird life here," Norma says. *"Ducks drop by on their way to the Arroyo, and birds stop in for a splash. I'm out here every day with my binoculars."*

This spread: The master bathroom and details from the property's fountains and reflecting pool; note the pass-through steam shower, the fireplace and sofa in the middle of the bathroom, the acres of tilework created by master artisans from Fez, and the intricately carved canopy over the master bathtub.

We've Heard of a Water Bed,
But This Is Ridiculous

Daniel "Rover" Singer and Cal Smith are the third owners of a unique piece of Americana, which they purchased a few years back. "Handmade house" isn't usually a descriptor, but this gem of a crib, located in Altadena, really was handmade, starting in 1937 by a man named Louis Steinhauser. Rover offers a witty crash course on the place. *"We don't know a lot about Louis, but he did leave a few interesting clues,"* says Rover. *"He built a core cabin, which took quite some time to finish because it's filled with lavishly detailed woodwork. He also built a garage, which he then converted into a master bedroom suite. The year carved into the plaster is 1944, which we believe is the year he finished this room."*

Steinhauser created this former garage for two activities, bathing and sleeping. *"But he developed an innovative concept that didn't catch on,"* Rover says. *"He made two rooms into one by placing a big, sunken Roman tub into the middle of the bedroom. There's a WC off to the side, and a little stall shower."* Loaded with practicality? No, it's not, says Rover. When one person is sleeping and the other is showering in the middle of the room, without so much as a how-de-do to separate the activities … well, it gets old.

"The sunken bath is made of Batchelder tile, which was considered old-fashioned in the 1940s," says Rover, noting the twelve-inch-square oak tree tiles, the jumbo abalone-shell soap dish and the built-in aquarium, which they haven't used because they're not sure it will hold water. There's also a shower bench that Steinhauser whittled. *"People ask us if we use the tub,"* says Rover. *"The answer is no. We don't have a hot water heater big enough to fill it. This is a very big tub. We're getting a flash hot water system, so then we'll see."*

This page: Folkloric carving decorates every wood surface in the Altadena home originally built by Louis Steinhauser; master suite has built-in carved wood closet and drawers chiseled with geometric shapes and flora.

Opposite page, clockwise from upper left: Sunken tiled tub and bench carved by Steinhauser; carved plaster wall niche proclaims the year 1944; large abalone shell serves as a soap holder; considered old-fashioned in the 1940s, this Batchelder tile may have been remaindered; the sunken tub with wall aquarium dominates the master bedroom/bathroom suite.

Agree to Disagree

"People see only the fountain when it's on, and when the fountain's not spraying, they only see a Jacuzzi," says homeowner Mark Puopolo. *"We designed the Jacuzzi so it could function as a set piece during a party or an event, but we still have a spa at the end of a very long day. And the booster jets are just great for those of us with bad backs."* When Mark and his partner, Chris Mullen, built the double-duty Jacuzzi/fountain in their Garfield Heights Victorian, they fitted the interior with glass tiles and had the exterior scored and crackled to create an instant patina. The adjacent chaise longues are fully occupied on Sundays until the coffee's gone and the paper's been read.

Mark and Chris restore historic residential properties for a living; they recently revived a house across the street and a Craftsman on Marengo. In addition to their 1886 Pasadena domicile they own a 1948 Palm Springs home, and they recently received landmark status for both. *"My family from Boston says, 'What? 1948 isn't old! Why are you preserving that?'"* says Mark. *"My feeling is, in 200 years, someone will be happy to walk through a 1948 house."*

Period materials like subway wall tiles, Carerra marble floor tiles and black grout make the bathroom crisp yet authentic. Slow and steady restoration (which actually involves watching paint dry) brings Mark and Chris great satisfaction. Except when they disagree. *"Chris wants everything to be original and look original. So do I, except when it comes to the bathtub,"* Mark says with a laugh. *"I want a pristine tub that looks clean. Bathtubs from the early 20th century tend to look a little dingy. I favor reglazing the tub, and Chris is against it. Because, of course, the risk is that once you start reglazing it, you have to keep reglazing from time to time."* So who won the argument? Chris. The tub was not reglazed, although it does have new hardware. *"And I'm the one who takes baths!"* Mark says. *"He owes me."*

Clockwise from upper left: Mark and Chris's dual-purpose spa/fountain; a beadboard-paneled anteroom leads outside from the Victorian house; "antiseptic white" subway tile and a Carerra marble floor complement the original clawfoot tub.

84

Over-the-Top Tile

Loren Tripp says the black-tiled bathroom confused her and her husband, Bruce Ryan, when they bought their canyon home. *"It was a very 1970s style,"* she says, *"which was unusual for the house. There weren't any other '70s references. The walls, ceiling and shower are tiled in this pillowy, Chiclet tile. It's quite over the top."* Visitors who grew up in the neighborhood were able to identify the tiles as coming from Claycroft Potteries. *"They also remarked on our heart-shaped tub, which made us wonder. Because we don't have a heart-shaped tub,"* recalls Loren. *"Our neighbor said, 'Look in the mirror.' Sure enough, in the mirror it's obviously a half-heart, and when you stand back, it's doubled. It's a funny, heart-shaped tub! We were so glad he spoke up."*

The Tripp-Ryans altered their master bath – one of six bathrooms – for comfort, getting rid of the pass-through shower, low sink and low toilet, which weren't particularly practical for this tall couple. A bathroom sitting room became a "his" bathroom, complete with a gentleman's urinal, heated towel rack and bamboo flooring.

Clockwise from upper left: Black-and-seafoam-green soaking tub in the Tripp-Ryan master bathroom; a new urinal for the man on the go; mirrors amplify the half-a-heart tub into illusory infinity; detail of the 1930s Claycroft tiles.

Bathing, Like It or Not

The owners of this Linda Vista home have a lovely pool that both Esther Williams and Nemo, the cartoon fish, would envy. The real-life family swims quite a bit in the summer months, especially Dad and the kids. *"They use the spa a lot,"* says Mom. They? What? Does Mom not want to get her hair wet, in this day and age? That's not it. *"No, I don't like it!"* she says. *"I have a water phobia. Which is silly, I know. I'm from an island, and I don't swim,"* she says with a sigh. When her kids were growing up here in Pasadena, she pretended to like the water, so as not to pass her fears on to them. But when her sons grew older, *"I showed my true colors,"* she says, ruefully. *"I got this phobia from my mother. She was afraid of the water, too, the poor lady. But, that was another era. You know, in California especially, I wanted my children to swim. It's important to be able to enjoy these things."* And so they do.

This page: In and around a Linda Vista pool and garden.

Opposite, clockwise from upper left: The San Gabriels peer down on David and Mary's Eaton Canyon pool; Moosie Simpson cools off; Carolyn and Craig Watson's swimming pool, restored with original brick and stone: the pool and spa behind David and Judy Brown's Greene & Greene home; the Spanish-Moorish four-lobed pool at the Yarivs' Arroyo house; drought-tolerant statice leans toward the Sezgins' saltwater lap pool.

Playing:
at home

There's a classic line attributed to a child (we're not mentioning names), who at age 8 was trying to make her escape from the house on a Saturday morning to join friends already outside playing hide-and-seek. Her mother called from the kitchen, *"Did you finish your chores?"* With one foot out the door, and a confident grasp on the way the world was supposed to work, she yelled back, *"Mom – you're the Mom, you do the chores. I'm the kid. I play."*

I'm the kid. I play. Sounds about right. Fredrich Froebel, a German philosopher and educator born in 1782 and the originator, in 1837, of the concept of the kindergarten (children's garden), was the first to describe play as a child's work. For his kindergarten, Froebel designed a series of simple playthings – balls, blocks, colored tiles, rings and sticks – called "Froebel Gifts," which were to be presented to young children to encourage their creative play. Froebel's studies of the natural world led him to believe that somewhere within the teeming complexities of nature were simple principles, and that play inspired by the geometric shapes of his "gifts" invited a child to participate in, and become privy to, nature's principles. If you are among the millions of children who played with the smooth, blond wooden blocks that became a standard of the American kindergarten and child's bedroom, you have Herr Froebel to thank. If your brother delighted in kicking down the elaborate structures you made, talk to your mother and leave us out of it.

Far more interesting (at least to us) than the resentment you've harbored against your brother these last thirty years is the through-line from Froebel to Frank Lloyd Wright. It is well documented that Wright, a man neither shy about his own genius nor noted for his glowing accolades of others, was profoundly influenced by his youthful play with the twenty Froebel Gifts given him by his progressive mother, who purchased them at the Philadelphia Exposition. *"The maple wood blocks … are in my fingers to this day,"* Wright wrote in his autobiography. Other of the Froebel Gifts – colorful papers, grids, sticks and tiny spherical joinings – inspired the young Wright and influenced his proportional system of design.

Let's leave Wright at play and return to the through-line, following it to the architecture of Richard Neutra, a student of Wright's and twenty-five years his junior. In her Taschen book, *Neutra*, architect and architectural historian Barbara Lamprecht says, while discussing Neutra's design philosophy of "biorealism" that emphasized the linking of the body and the mind, *"The theory provided a rationale for why people need physical contact with nature, even why they need to see the horizon. Embracing such a hypothesis was also one of the reasons Neutra went not just to America but specifically to warm, freedom-loving Southern California."*

And so he did, and so we are rich in examples of his residential architecture, including South Pasadena's Wilkins House, which we are lucky enough to include in these pages. Neutra's interest in the connection between health and the natural environment takes us back to the through-line, where we arrive at the present: the greening of contemporary

architecture. And here, with a tip of its hemp cap to Neutra and Wright, the current and future masters of sustainable residential architecture are settling in to the serious work of developing "green" homes for generations of children at play.

But for now, we're in beautiful Pasadena on a gorgeous day, so put down this book – it's not going anywhere – and go outside and play in the yard.

And take your sister with you.

– JAG

Clockwise, from above: Quincy (left) and Peter Ryan play knights in their Altadena yard; Arielle (left) and Alexandra Baptiste in their Prospect Park backyard with their friends on their trampoline.

"I cannot go to school today," said little Peggy Ann McKay. "I have the measles and the mumps, a gash, a rash, and purple bumps. My mouth is wet, my throat is dry, I'm going blind in my right eye…. "What's that? What's that you say? You say today is… Saturday? G'bye, I'm going out to play!"

– Shel Silverstein (1932-1999)

Between Kid and Grown-up

"When we're in the barn we feel a kind of safeness... like the feeling you get when you're a little kid and you're comfortable and safe. You're in a house – well, for my friends and me it's a barn, but we have a place where we don't have to worry about anything... because we have so much in our lives that is crazy and intense with high school and life. We're kind of connected to the house, but we are separate. Once in a while, my mom will even call from the house and say, 'This is the house calling.' She really, really gives us our space, which is so nice. It is sort of exactly where we are in life... we're 'at home' and my mom is right there in the house but we're still out in the barn on our own. There's just so much to think about with what we have to do and what we're gonna do and what we need to do and what we didn't do.

"We're definitely between being kids and being grown-ups. I've surrounded myself with a lot of friends who can still act like little kids while being teenagers. All of my friends can still really play! A few months ago we went to the park and had a baby-powder fight. I think it is important to be able to play that way when you're this age.

"I remember loving to get dirty when I was a little kid. Once when I was pretty young, my friend Erin and I dug a huge hole in our rose garden and took a mud bath. Playing was messy back then, and it's what I still like... I guess it's letting go. I know some grown-ups that are playful – very few really, and I always notice them. But I feel kind of determined to be one of those parents who can really get down on their knees and play. It's almost like when I play and do silly things – I kind of feel like I'm proving someone wrong, because there are so many people who tell us what we need to do – who will talk us out of having fun like that – so it becomes harder and harder to be able to do it. I know how easy it is to stop having fun, so I think we do a good job of trying to grow up but still be able to play."

– Darah Gillum, age 17, South Pasadena High School student

Left: Darah Gillum (above left) lives in a small South Pasadena bungalow with her mother, Chris Jansen-Gillum. Jansen-Gillum fell in love with the property because of its charm, location, affordability and, most of all, its ramshackle barn, which she thought would make the perfect teenage hangout. She dressed it up with an old sofa and chairs, a vintage chandelier and a collection of board games, and sure enough, it's become command central for Darah and her friends.

Right: Classic backyard play is the cornerstone of Pasadena family life. Clockwise, from upper left: a vintage-style tricycle in a San Marino yard; Emery Mann and friend race through the lawns surrounding her family's meticulously restored Richard Neutra-designed house in South Pasadena; Jack Williamson in his family's San Pasqual backyard; Laura Davich gets ready for her dad's pitch in their Prospect Park yard.

Overleaf: clockwise, from lower left: Color and fantasy in Logan Criley's Linda Vista bedroom; Lukas Hutzler and guitar in his Sierra Madre home; Laura and Hannah Davich's feminine room is large enough to accommodate play, homework and sleeping; Emery Mann (right) and friend Maggie Nutley, throw many a tea party in her airy, clean-lined playroom.

Catherine Sezgin was in complete opposition to Gameboy, until she discovered that her son Evren was an expert player. *"It seemed hypocritical to not let him play at home. If a guy knows and plays Gameboy with all his friends, it is not going away."*

Clockwise from upper left: Erin and Evren Sezgin and their Gameboys; a media room that's well used by a Pasadena family's teenage daughters and their friends; the game room in Norma and Gary Cowles's historic Bertram Goodhue-designed home.

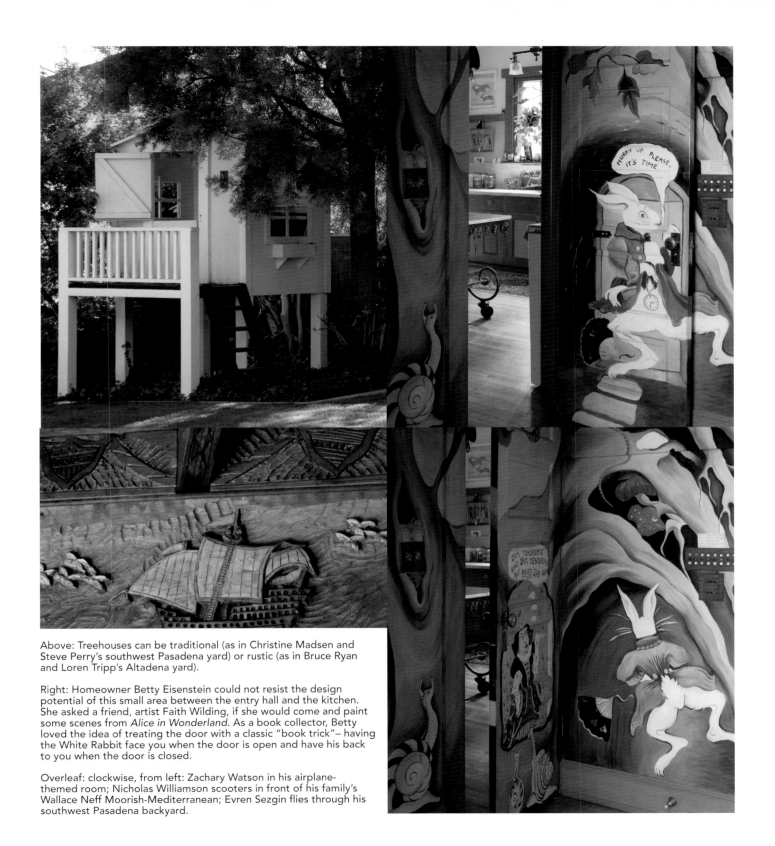

Above: Treehouses can be traditional (as in Christine Madsen and Steve Perry's southwest Pasadena yard) or rustic (as in Bruce Ryan and Loren Tripp's Altadena yard).

Right: Homeowner Betty Eisenstein could not resist the design potential of this small area between the entry hall and the kitchen. She asked a friend, artist Faith Wilding, if she would come and paint some scenes from *Alice in Wonderland*. As a book collector, Betty loved the idea of treating the door with a classic "book trick"– having the White Rabbit face you when the door is open and have his back to you when the door is closed.

Overleaf: clockwise, from left: Zachary Watson in his airplane-themed room; Nicholas Williamson scooters in front of his family's Wallace Neff Moorish-Mediterranean; Evren Sezgin flies through his southwest Pasadena backyard.

Wannap ay ? et sgoouta

dplay.CanIgoplayatMat

hew's house?Wannapla

yfort?Thebigkidswon'tle

meplay.Let'splaymonste

.Whowantstoplaythatst

pidgame *off* thatTV

ndgo*out* nd*play*!Le

splaydoctor. thesaidv

'dplay*my*gameafterwep

ayedhisgame.I'llteachyo

uhowtoplay.Putyourplay

lotheson.Let'splayhous

andnoplayingrough!

Working:
at home

If play is the work of children, then work is… well, work is the work of adults. There's no getting around it – almost all of us work. We work because we need to earn money; we work because something has engaged our attention or engorged our passion (yes, that too provides gainful employment for some, though we'd direct you to the *other* valley for that discussion). But you know what we mean – work is, of necessity, central to our lives. Let's be truthful here: Even if it is not about the money, even if you've got some real dough tucked away, it is still sort of about the money – we are, as a species, set apart from other animals by that big frontal lobe that tells us (among other things) that we need to plan for the day when we will no longer be able to do the work we are able to do now. Besides, we are naturally inclined to be industrious, and also, we need to eat. We're not talking avarice, you understand, but industry: idle hands/devil's playground and all that funny business. We accomplish tasks that fulfill needs, and we get paid, or we get praised, or we learn something and feel satisfied for having done so. There's a real "*atta boy!*" attached to doing good work, and we are, none of us, immune from appreciating praise for a job well done.

There is the potential for great pleasure in work. There is also the potential for big, fat irrefutable headaches, office politics, vending machines, fear of the boss peering over your shoulder when you're answering e-mail, boredom and, according to *Money* magazine, a median commute of 20.9 minutes each way for Pasadenans, with 17.9% of us enduring a commute of forty-five minutes or longer. Say we split the difference and consider a thirty-minute commute to and from work each day – we did the math, and that's 240 hours, or ten days per year, spent commuting to and from work. For the curious or masochistic among you, spin that out for ten or twenty years and see where it gets you.

All of which is to say that there is much to be said for working at home. It has been with us for hundreds of years. Cottage industries during the 18th and 19th centuries focused on textiles: lacework, sewing and weaving, which took place in the home as a byproduct of farming. The Industrial Revolution carried the rural poor into the cities to work in new (albeit dangerous) factories. But the popularization of the computer, the internet and the relentless march down the information highway have influenced not only a rebirth of interest inworking at home but the capacity to telecommute and exchange digital information whilst sitting at your desk in your jammies. A friend of ours, freelancing for many years in the magazine racket, was fond of saying her epitaph was going to be: *Here Lies Celeste – She never took a job she couldn't do in her pajamas.* In the 2000 Census (the most recent available), of the approximate half-million people in California who worked at home, 67.5% of them were between the ages of 25 and 59, the prime working years.

Among the Baby Boomers – born between 1946 and 1964 – the oldest are eyeballing retirement, and, might we add, considering setting up consulting businesses they intend to run out of their homes. But many of the youngest Boomers are in their early to mid-40s and, thanks to the

phenomenon of delaying childbirth, are still in the thick of raising young families.

Some years ago, when dropping my young son at school every morning, I would say, *"Have fun. Work hard."* I don't recall ever thinking about the phrase, it just was what I said, like *"Goodnight, sweet dreams."* After a couple of years of saying this each morning, I came to realize it was something of a mantra: something I might just as readily apply to my days as a mother, working at home and looking for balance throughout the long, sometimes sweet, sometimes demanding days: Have fun. Work hard.

– JAG

Altadenan Dana Hursey, a commercial photographer, lives in a 1,344-square-foot Gregory Ain Park Planned Home built in 1946. Hursey and his partner, real estate appraiser Jeremy Cowin, are both self-employed and work out of offices in their home. While they have done some thoughtful remodeling, the house retains its original modest square footage yet feels airy, bright and even spacious. The fact that both men could create offices to suit their professional needs begs two questions: Why commute to an office? And why pay for office space when that money might be used to develop the property they own?

Says Hursey, *"I think you're built one way or the other. You either love working from your home, or you hate it because you feel like you can never get away from it. I would find it hard to give up the convenience. My time is my own. If I want to get a little work done on a Saturday afternoon, I can do it without having to get in the car and go somewhere, or I can check up on something at ten o'clock at night if I want to."* The fact that all of his photographic work is digital precludes the need for a darkroom. If he does need to make prints, he has that capacity in his home office, and the finished garage serves as a studio when needed. Hursey completed the first phase of remodeling before moving in, tearing out a second bathroom to make the office space large enough. The next and final phase of the remodeling will include a pool and cabana-style office for Jeremy, allowing his current office to become a part of an expanded master bedroom suite.

Left page, clockwise from bottom: An antique desk and chair pay homage to the schoolhouse roots of Suzanne and Michael Criley's 1880s house in Linda Vista; Dana Hursey and Jeremy Cowin make every inch count in the offices in their compact Altadena midcentury modern.

This page, top: David Brown, executive director of Descanso Gardens, works often in the office in his Greene & Greene home, where he's long pursued his love of tropical aquariums; bottom: Ed and Marcia Nunnery have figured out how to work separately but together at home in southwest Pasadena.

Many Little Shrines

The backyard garden of illustrator and screenwriter Michael Criley is a lush, surprising wilderness that evokes a secret, abandoned compound complete with what appear to be the ruins of an ancient foundation – a sort of a Roanoke, he says, referring to the Lost Colony, the first English colony of the New World, which was twice settled in the late 16th century and twice abandoned under mysterious circumstances. Criley describes this extraordinary space – with its ruined wall and foundation and the detritus of previous generations coaxed into subtle and not so subtle display – as a sanitarium for the friends, real and imaginary, who might be drawn to it for its solemnity and opportunity for contemplation. For Criley, who works in his home studio, and his family, there is great awareness of the shards of living produced by the generations of inhabitants of this property: a schoolhouse in the 19th century and, since then, a home. Inside Criley's studio are artifacts and historic photographs from research laboratories, hospitals, schools, asylums and sanitariums – and the gravitas of all these institutions is somehow reflected in the wild garden setting that borders his studio and the back of his home.

Michael, Suzanne and their son, Logan, all love the garden, with its many little shrines, both reverent and irreverent. The objects excavated from the garden provide the support for a changing narrative as Criley, a self-described "completely unreliable narrator" (in the spirit, perhaps, of Beat Generation novelist William S. Burroughs), embellishes details and adds and subtracts from his archaeological finds as he takes on the role of storyteller, offering up a sort of fractured allegory that can be retold at the teller's whim. This, he says, is a compelling lesson to his son about the revisionist nature of history: Anything you see in a museum should be observed through a healthy lens of skepticism; anything you read in a history book is just one person's view of the tales told and footprints described. History is not static, it changes over time – like a garden.

Left: The porch outside Michael Criley's backhouse studio sets the stage for his seriously imaginative work.

Right: Illustrative and excavated items in the Criley family's Linda Vista yard, including an elevated playhouse (upper right).

A Playroom for Working

"I've never particularly liked traditional office space," says psychoanalyst Bonnie Saland. *"Working at home feels very, very comfortable to me."* Clients come to her home office via a private entrance, and her appointments are convened in a gracious, personal space surrounded by greenery – an environment Saland believes to be appropriate to her contemporary version of psychoanalysis. The traditional image of the psychoanalytic office is that of the blank screen, but Saland's office is certainly not that. As she says, *"Some people find this office too chaotic, and it stands to reason that I might not be the right match for them."*

For clients who are interested, Saland does sand play as an adjunct therapy. Modern therapeutic sand play is the descendent of the original work of Dr. Margaret Lowenfeld, a child psychoanalyst in England in the 1920s, and Dora Kalff, who collaborated with Lowenfeld and also worked with famed Swiss psychiatrist Carl Jung in the 1950s. Originally developed for children, sand play is now also used with adults – it is likely to be most useful to adults who are interested in their own unconscious imagery and are willing to be playful. In sand play therapy, the participants use miniature figures and objects to create stories in a sand tray, thereby facilitating participation in the unconscious world while becoming less inhibited by conscious awareness.

You've achieved success in your field when you don't know whether what you are doing is work or play.
— Warren Beatty

The secret of being miserable is to have the leisure to bother about whether you are happy or not. The cure is occupation.
— George Bernard Shaw

Work consists of whatever a body is obliged to do, and play consists of whatever a body is not obliged to do.
— Mark Twain, *The Adventures of Tom Sawyer*

Telegram to a friend who had just become a mother after a prolonged pregnancy: *Good work, Mary. We all knew you had it in you.*
— Dorothy Parker

No matter how big or soft or warm your bed is, you still have to get out of it.
— Grace Slick

Cessation of work is not accompanied by cessation of expenses.
— Cato the Elder

I don't have anything against work. I just figure, why deprive somebody who really loves it?
— Dobie Gillis

"What is wonderful about working at home is the accessibility. What is challenging about it is the accessibility. It requires that you train the mind and become singularly directed with your work. I don't distinguish the work of gardening from the work of homemaking or cooking or writing or child rearing. My work is very much one and the same as my life."
— Karen Miller, a Pasadena mother, wife, Zen Buddhist priest and author

Upper left: Elaine Carhartt's tilework surrounds the entrance to her studio, which occupies a converted garage.

Left: Examples of Elaine Carhartt's ceramic scupltures and linoleum block and prints.

107

When Play Becomes Work

Television and film composer Marty Davich started playing piano at age 4 and recalls the exceptional access to music in the Phoenix public schools. *"I played trumpet in sixth grade, I played tuba in the marching band, I played bass in the high school orchestra, I sang in the choirs and I got to arrange for the choirs,"* he says. Because of that experience, he now volunteers with other musician buddies to play at local public schools and expose kids to music, which he describes as his first language, noting that he could read music before he could read English. He's been a TV composer for about 25 years, writing music for *Beverly Hills 90210*, various miniseries and every single episode of *ER*; he also enjoys scoring for film.

Working at home enables Marty to have the family life that is so vital to him. This means a family dinner every night, no matter how busy he may be; it means being there for homework and a kiss goodnight. He credits working at home with being able to be a present parent while managing a very busy career.

Clockwise, from top: Marty Davich making the backyard commute from work to home with daughter Laura; Jacob Davich working at playing; Jacob's guitar collection is the heart of his room.

When Work Becomes Play

So when does the chore of practicing an instrument turn into the joy of playing that instrument? It's hard to pinpoint that transition, but while all three of the Davich children took piano lessons, *"Jacob is the one who is just possessed,"* says his father, Marty. In addition to rarely being seen around the house without his Fender Stratocaster, 16-year-old Jacob is also a successful actor, a career that came to him almost accidentally, with both parents initially resistant to the idea. (You can see him as the young Howard Hughes in *The Aviator*.)

The Method of Painting

Milo Reice, below left, tells us he was not yet 5 when he went to the Metropolitan Museum of Art in New York and knew he wanted to paint. His work has always been most influenced by artists and paintings. If a collector visits his studio and likes his work, *"then great… it makes me feel on the top of the world, particularly if it is a great collector, but very seldom, if ever, would it make me steer my work in a direction."* He is still influenced by what his mother told him when he was a boy, which is now what he tells young people: Whether you are an artist or a financier, you have to do what you love.

"I used to relate more directly to the characters in my paintings," says Milo. *"In 1979-'80 I did a painting of Faust and the devil, and while I was painting the devil, I dressed as a devil for a month straight. It was the punk era and that was a part of it – I think it was method acting for painting. Today, it happens in a different way. While I'm involved in the production of a painting, it is as though I am one-on-one with it. But as soon as a painting is done, it's done, and I'm off to something else."*

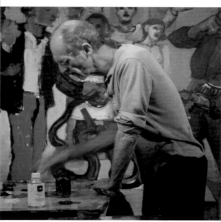

Right: Milo Reice's painting, *Stop Back from Egypt*, is based on the central panel of a Holy Family triptych: Mary is seated on the roadside with the young Jesus holding a crown of thorns that he is using as a basketball hoop. Joseph is present behind them, and the lion is a symbol of majesty.

Painter Ray Turner on Works in Progress

"I've become almost more confident that I'm actually doing something that is legitimate… that is real. You evaluate and grow and learn and become more circumspect. I work in oil, and it is a very organic process. I may do ten or twenty different paintings, one over the next on the same canvas – one day it's a landscape and the next day it's some architectural thing. I may have lost some good paintings that way, and maybe I photographed it, but maybe not. And there can be frustration when a gallery comes to see the work and decides to have a show, and maybe they've even shot the image and printed the announcement. But they come back and they want to see the painting they'd seen under way and… it's gone. I mean, it's there somewhere. So I know it can be frustrating for the gallery, but my commitment is to try to make the best painting I can. I may even ruin a painting, but I think the willingness or the courage or the stupidity or whatever causes you to say, no, it's not good enough. The challenge is to keep trying to figure out when a painting is working. And inevitably there is an hour when it just comes together – whether it's six months or two hours – the magic is when it is there – I can see, feel it, taste it. It's just there."

Below: Ray Turner in his Madison Heights studio.

Opposite page: Ray Turner's works in progress.

Lately Pasadena mixed-media artist Jennifer Frank, above, has been experimenting with printing her photos on fabric, a technique that seems a natural melding of two of her talents: black-and-white photography and fashion design (as Jennifer Joanou, she was a clothing retailer and wholesaler in L.A.). She also works in a form known as a "visual journal," which uses words and images in a book format. She incorporates paper, paint, rubber stamps, fabric, pages torn from magazines – whatever strikes her fancy. Sometimes the work is derived from artistic interests that already are in place, and sometimes they lead to entirely new art projects. In fact, Frank says visual journaling can be an excellent warm-up for many artists, who may work on their journals before focusing on their other art. Her youngest daughter, Stella, often joins her mom in the studio to work on her own visual journal.

The Work of George Ellery Hale

We were thrilled to be granted permission to include in these pages some glorious images of the Hale Solar Observatory, which is located in Pasadena. It is an exceptional example of scientific and architectural history, once deeded to, and then abandoned by, the Carnegie Foundation, and now in the capable hands of private citizens. We've based some of the scientific information that follows on a discussion with Don Nicholson, who appears with his colleague, Gale Gant, in these photos taken on a beautiful summer afternoon. Any information that does not conform to Nicholson's exacting standards is unquestionably the fault of the writer, an admirer of George Ellery Hale, and of his observatory, but not, alas, a scientist herself.

Nicholson has had a lifelong interest in astronomy. A retired optical systems engineer and current president of the Mount Wilson Observatory Association, he is the son of Seth Nicholson, staff astronomer at the Mount Wilson Observatory from 1915 to 1957, where, among other significant achievements, he discovered four of the moons of Jupiter. In June 2007, Don Nicholson received a commendation from the city of Pasadena for his "tremendous contributions to the Mount Wilson Observatory and to the city of Pasadena." A wry and modest man, Nicholson first assures us that it isn't true, then suggests that if they are offering such an accolade to him, they must be giving them out on a weekly basis. But, when pressed to accept the honor, he is willing to go so far as to say, *"If I have accomplished anything, the credit largely goes to Hale: If it weren't for him, my parents would not have been in Pasadena and I would not have had the opportunity to grow up in an environment that was influenced in great measure by him."*

The Pasadena firm of Johnson Kaufman and Coate designed the Hale Solar Observatory in 1924, with grounds by landscape architect Beatrix Farrand, the only woman among the founding members of the American Society of Landscapers. An internationally recognized scientist, George Ellery Hale was influential in civic and international activities by the time he commissioned the observatory, which became his office and workshop. With its stone bas-relief above the entrance and second bas-relief over the library fireplace, the building pays tribute to Hale's interest in Egyptology. Hale was exceptional for his day in his ability to design and fabricate instruments needed for particular observations in his own machine shop, which is located in the basement. Visiting the observatory, we experienced the quiet thrill that we recall from childhood visits to Jefferson's Monticello, where, while viewing rooms from behind the velvet rope, we desperately wanted to enter each room and sit at the desk or hold the tea cup that he had held. The intimacy one feels with history at the observatory is due to the intimacy of the space itself, which we felt acutely when there to watch the dome being opened to accommodate the telescope. We walked among rooms containing Hale's personal papers, tools and typewriter, which remain much as they might have been when last he used them.

Hale had a long and distinguished career, in which his observatory played a significant role. He first detected the solar magnetic field in 1908 at the Mount Wilson Observatory, and in 1914 he made the observation that the sunspots of the northern and southern hemispheres reversed polarity every eleven years. But it was not until 1925, when he had his own laboratory, that Hale and collaborator Seth Nicholson finally published the Hale-Nicholson Law, confirming that while the magnetic polarity of sunspots flips every eleven years, the entire pattern repeats every 22 years. *"That,"* says Nicholson, *"was probably the most significant piece of science to emerge from the Hale lab."*

Hale's interest in astronomy was with him all his life. His father, a wealthy Chicago businessman, bought him his first telescope at 14 and built him his own observatory on their property once he entered college. He went on to become a driving force in astronomy, building four of the world's largest telescopes, Mount Wilson's and Palomar's among them, and founding the National Research Council. He was also a man of considerable civic engagement. A great friend of Henry Huntington, he is known to have influenced Huntington's decision to endow his famous Art Gallery and Library. He was a member of the Pasadena Planning Commission and lobbied successfully to build Pasadena's distinguished Civic Auditorium, City Hall and Central Library. With Robert Millikan and Alfred Noyes, he oversaw the transformation of Throop Polytechnic into what we casually refer to today as Caltech. Upon retiring from the directorship of the Mount Wilson Observatory, Hale is said to have chosen Pasadena as the home for his own observatory after noting the favorable conditions present during the day. We also have heard that he was loathe to be too far from lunch at Caltech's Athenaeum. In either event, the history of Pasadena is richer for Hale having done his remarkable work there.

Left page, clockwise from top: Don Nicholson in the open observatory dome; Nicholson, foreground, and Gale Gant; details from the observatory; the front door to the observatory.

Above: Detail, over the observatory door, of the bas-relief of Egyptian pharoh Akhenaton and his god, Aten, the visible disc of the sun.

Following spread: Left page, details from the Hale Observatory interior; right page, Don Nicholson and Gale Gant prepare the telescope for a solar observation.

Collecting:
at home

There are as many kinds of collectors as there are things to collect: For every collector of plein air art, there is a collector of cookbooks; for every man, woman or child who collects baseball memorabilia, you will find an equal number who collect menus from burger shacks up and down the California coast. We collect pottery, cocktail shakers, children's toys, erotica, exotica, matchbooks, airplane propellers, trailers, first editions, every imaginable kind of art, photography, finely wrought miniatures, sterling creamers, sea shells and fiberglass reindeer – to name but a few collectibles.

Among collectors, there are subcategories that divide us, and not only by the resources we are able to muster. With a nod to Swedish naturalist Carl Linnæus, who gave us the method for classifying living things (kingdom, phylum, class, order, family, genus, species), collectors are classified into those who collect with an air of serendipity – Pez dispensers today, Victoriana tomorrow – and those who stalk their prey for months, years, a lifetime perhaps, searching for that British Guiana 1c magenta or that Swedish Three Skilling Banco yellow stamp. And while we may very well be from the same family, when it comes to genus, we are either hunters or gatherers; as for species, well, it's back to the matter of whatever floats your boat. (And, yes, we had to look up the Linnæus reference, since we could hardly remember the order back in high school, and it's been a few years.)

In this wonderful place we call home, we have flora in the Arroyo to collect and press into books to mark days spent in that beautiful, still-wild place in our city; antiques stores for every taste and pocketbook; houses of architectural significance that are themselves collectors' items; and a glorious legacy of collecting, starting with Henry Huntington. We should not forget that in addition to founding Pacific Electric Railway, Huntington was a true collector who began by amassing the rare books and manuscripts that now reside in the library bearing his name, and whose home, designed by Los Angeles architects Myron Hunt and Elmer Grey and known today as the Huntington Gallery, houses British and French 18th- and 19th-century art, objets d'art and furnishings, and is the pride of San Marino. In Pasadena, the Norton Simon Museum became home to the "Blue Four" modernist collection of German expatriate art dealer and collector Galka Scheyer in 1953 when UCLA, the initial recipient of the collection, failed to build a museum to display it. Go Pasadena!

In our very unscientific survey of this city of more than 146,000 (plus our neighbors in San Marino, South Pasadena, Altadena and environs), we can tell you that a lot of smart, interesting people are inspired to collect something, and while, in our wayward youth, we used to think sneaking a peek into people's medicine cabinets was a thrill, we now know that was nothing compared to actually being invited to check out these collections. Each and every one of them surprised us, intrigued us and made us happy as can be.

– JAG

The Architect as Collector

Architect Jean Maurice Moulene collects the art, furnishings and objects that suit his eclectic tastes. He is particularly interested in the work of furniture designer and architect Eileen Gray. Gray, born to an aristocratic family in Ireland in 1878, lived in Paris in the early 1900s and is now recognized for her significant influence on design during the first half of the 20th century. Two of her Transat chairs (below and at right) are seen in Moulene's loft at Mission Meridian Village in South Pasadena. Gray created the chairs in the 1920s for the first villa she designed on the Côte d'Azur, and Moulene found them in an antiques store in Europe. He describes this chair (along with its well-known Charles Eames counterpart) as exceptionally comfortable as well as beautiful. A 1940s typewriter table sits next to one of the chairs in Moulene's beautifully composed living room; a vintage Shaw-Walker office chair from the '50s was a find from a local flea market. The folding camp-style bench, found in an antiques store here, is much appreciated for its comfort, shape and the fact that, as Moulene says, *"You can fold it up and put it in your pocket."* But its greatest pleasure is revealed when the sun comes through the sliding balcony door and the perforated seat casts its wonderful shadow across the concrete floor.

"I think it is very important to mix true American and true European design," says Moulene. *"I like the space to be eclectic. It can be boring to have only one style in a place – it's much more exciting is to marry one style to another."* An unabashed fan of Westerns, he cites John Ford films and John Wayne as important icons during his childhood in France. A painting by Patrick Altman (son of filmmaker Robert Altman) called "Go West"– paint on film, mounted over a white background – hangs at the base of the stairs. And Moulene, who sought a Frederic Remington sculpture for many years, treasures the large Remington bronze he finally scored at a silent auction in Santa Monica.

Above, lower right: Jean Maurice Moulene was particularly taken with the quality of the light from this Murano glass table lamp. *"The purity and color of the glass is really amazing,"* he says. *"It changes from green to white when it is lit… it is kind of magical."*

Above: Dana Hursey visited a Gregory Ain home that was on the market in Mar Vista. It had a central hallway with a sliding wall that could be used to bisect one of the two bedrooms to create a third room when needed. So the decision to include a sliding pocket panel in the hallway of Dana's and his partner Jeremy's Ain-designed Park Planned Home in Altadena evokes a modular quality that is very much in keeping with the spirit of the original design. During the renovation, they wanted the space to accommodate a significant piece of art, and so it does: The Warhol illustration by Kamran Moojedi is a piece Dana coveted for a decade before purchasing it and hanging it to such great effect.

Closed, the panel hides the laundry area and aligns side-by-side with the oversize digital image of Andy Warhol. Opened, it slides along a horizontal mechanism and over a pocket deep enough to safely hold the illustration while providing access to the laundry facilities.

Above right: Jennifer and Scott Frank began collecting black-and-white photography early in their marriage, and the image of Katharine Hepburn by famed photographer George Hurrell was one of the first significant pieces they bought. Jennifer, an accomplished photographer herself, was attracted to the photo for its exquisite iconic rendition of Hepburn. They began with the intent of developing a collection, but, as Jennifer says, *"It became more about loving a given photograph."* The fundamental rule for this couple's collecting method: They both have to love the photograph for it to go from interest to purchase.

Above: At the end of a summer of shell collecting, the Franks' daughter Stella returns all but her favorite shells to the beach.

119

Above & right: The Linda Vista homeowners arrived in this country from their native Sri Lanka as a young married couple, intending to be here briefly for career purposes. Twenty-nine years later, they have raised their family in Pasadena and acquired beautiful pieces locally and shipped family pieces and other antiques from Sri Lanka and Hawaii, where her parents had settled. They collect what strikes their joint fancy, but each has found things, such as perfume bottles and snuff jars, that have become personal collectibles.

The Thai monk (above; next page, top left & center bottom), with hands pressed together in greeting, bids visitors to enter the shingled English country–style home. Discovered here in Pasadena, the mid-19th-century, gilt-clad bronze was coveted by the husband – unusual, said his wife, as she is typically the one who envisions adding pieces to their home. But her husband was insistent, saying, *"It is so beautiful, and it has so much peace in it."* So he and his son rearranged the house to accommodate the large, graceful and welcoming monk.

Most of the porcelain (next page, top right) is Sri Lankan blue and white – showing the influence of the Chinese as well as the early Dutch colonization before Sri Lanka was ceded to the British in 1815.

This ox cart (next page, center right), purchased at a modest price in Sri Lanka, reminded the wife of a common sight in her childhood. *"A family would travel in it – a man and his wife and children, and always, you would see a little boy on the small back seat with his legs dangling,"* she says. *"I saw one in a little seaside antiques place, and I said to my husband, 'Look – it is only two hundred dollars.' But then, of course, it had to be shipped in a container, and my husband was a bit horrified at the time, but I said it was wonderful, because everything else we bought would fit in the container, and it was as though it would ship for free. It turned out to be very good, because we were able to send many beautiful things back here to America, things we would never get at such a good price today."*

Opposite, bottom left: This is what was called a "what-not" in Sri Lanka – as if to say you might use it to display whatever you choose. It was a ramshackle piece in two parts on the floor of a shop, and the couple purchased it and began to have it cleaned. It was covered with a thick dark finish that began to stink horribly as the scrubbing with coconut husk commenced, but eventually a beautiful wood with much inlay began to appear, and the ornate display piece has become a treasured family heirloom.

The Thrill of the Hunt

Bob Kneisel, retired from his profession as an environmental economist, started collecting stamps and rocks as a child with his twin brother. His father was an amateur archaeologist who took his sons to search for Indian arrowheads in the semi-rural area around their Louisville, Kentucky, home. Kneisel credits the early observational skills he developed for fostering some of his later success at swap meets – during his 24 years in a Pasadena bungalow, he has done a great deal of scavenging at our famous flea markets. Already a swap meet habitué who collected Mission furniture and art pottery *"while the getting was good and they were still somewhat reasonable,"* Kneisel was in the Pasadena Antique Center when a miniature pot metal (an inexpensive metal alloy used to make castings) silhouette of New York City caught his eye. Before long he found other miniatures at the Rose Bowl and PCC flea markets, and his next collection was born. *"They were cheap when I started,"* he says. *"I love architecture, and it was potentially infinite – I'll never run out of buildings. Fifteen or so years ago we started the Souvenir Building Collectors Society and have a membership – many of them architects – of about 200 people. We don't take ourselves too seriously, but it is a fraternity of sorts."*

As a kid, Bob Kneisel marveled at a clock in his grandmother's basement. Actually, it was a cut-off propeller with a clock in its center. After his time in the Air Force, he was in Riverside as a graduate student and was unsuccessfully scouring antiques stores for a propeller. Eventually he realized that the wind machines used by fruit growers to prevent frost in the fields used old World War II wooden propellers as their blades. As the farmers replaced the old wooden props, Kneisel bought and refinished them, then sold them to pilots, antiques stores and restaurants. He helped put himself through graduate school on the proceeds.

The Art of Collecting Wine

David and his wife, Margaret, have long been interested in wine, but it was not until they constructed the Pasadena home in which they now live with their two daughters that they built their beautiful wine cellar. *"In our first house, we had what I refer to as a decorative wine rack,"* says David, *"maybe 40 bottles behind glass in the kitchen, and you couldn't really drink them because they were pretty much cooked."* They decided to build a dark, temperature-controlled room in their new house, even though, as David says, they didn't know much about wine. Once they built the cellar, they went to Mission Wine in South Pasadena and embarked on their education with a mixed case each month or so: a red from Chile, a white Burgundy from France, a German Riesling and so on. The criterion was simple – did they like it or not? They discovered that they enjoyed a wide range of wines, and it was time to begin stocking the 2,800-bottle cellar.

David says his collection fits within three categories: wines to drink every day, those to cellar for the near future for family dinners or parties and, finally, wines that will benefit from being cellared for ten to fifteen years. Each must share one essential trait: that its taste truly reflects the region from which it comes. *"If we are drinking a French Bordeaux, we don't want it to taste like a California Cabernet,"* he says. As a kid David collected stamps, and he likens his experience with wine to that of his childhood interest: *"Stamps were interesting because they represented particular times in history and different places in the world; our wine collection has a very similar feel to me. I may have a southern Rhône Châteauneuf-du-Pape, or a Spanish Rioja, or if we're having an Italian dinner, I'll pull out an Italian Brunello or Barolo. Most recently I'm learning about Burgundy. It is very complex; I'm reading articles and tasting, and I'm starting to get it."*

David uses cellartracker.com, a free online service developed by a Microsoft retiree with a passion for wine. We've taken a look and found it accessible and easy to use, whether you are tracking two bottles or 20,000 – it's a lot like tracking a stock you're considering buying, but with less risk and an always-delicious payoff. David describes it as an internet commune with 20,000 to 30,000 users. You enter your wines into the system, keep track of which ones you have on hand, pull out what you want to drink and read what others have to say about a wine (perhaps learning how long it is best decanted or whether it is beginning to age past its peak); you can download all your information into Excel and have a hard copy if you want. David likes cellartracker.com because you hear what nonprofessional people have to say: *"Professional wine reviewers might describe a wine by saying it tastes 'inky.' What can that possibly mean? But if somebody says, 'This wine is really good, with a taste of cherry,' I know what to do with that."*

Okay, so perhaps wine software is not so romantic as Ingrid Bergman and Cary Grant clinging to each other inside the dank, scary wine cellar as Nazi Claude Rains approaches in Alfred Hitchcock's 1946 film *Notorious*, but it's a heck of a way to track that 1946 Chateau Lafleur Pomerol Bordeaux you've been dreaming about.

Clockwise from the top: In David and Margaret's wine cellar; storage for individual bottles and entire cases; a painting in their bedroom by Ray Turner. Margaret saw the two ottomans tucked under a table in an antiques shop on Melrose and realized they'd work in her bedroom, even before learning they were by renowned Milanese designer Gio Ponti.

Playful Collecting

Sam and Betty Eisenstein's sense of fun is inescapable. *"The idea of formality,"* says Betty, *"is something we like to avoid."* But while they may be having a grand old time amid their toys and books and textiles, a strong sense of style and wit is also present throughout their home. And there is plenty to gaze upon. They've been in their Sylvanus Marston Tudor Craftsman in Pasadena's Prospect Park for 30 years, and they've been collecting for longer than that. Our first inclination was to imagine the Eisensteins' focus on toys as the result of some deep memory of childhood – can we all say, "Rosebud"? (We certainly did.) But the story is far richer, and it speaks to many Californians who were here in the 1960s and were familiar with the activist artist and writer Corita Kent, a nun in the Immaculate Heart of Mary community and an unconventional art teacher at Immaculate Heart College in Los Angeles. Sam Eisenstein, who was then (as now) teaching at Los Angeles City College, met Sister Corita in the '60s, and they developed a weekly routine of walking in the gardens at Immaculate Heart. Through her, Sam met her early mentor, Sister Magdalene Mary. *"Maggie was an extraordinary woman in her own right,"* says Betty. *"She amassed a very large collection of folk art that she secreted in the basement at Immaculate Heart, and Sam would visit her collection with her."* When Immaculate Heart found itself in financial need, Sister Mary Magdalene put the collection up for auction. *"Some of the most incredible pieces went to others with more funds, but we bought what we could,"* says Betty. *"And that was our start as collectors."*

This page and opposite: The art, antique toys, children's books, textiles and furnishings in Sam and Betty Eisenstein's collection.

Above lower left: This organ, a signed piece made by Italian organ and harmonium maker G. Bacigalupo probably in the early 20th century, was part of Sister Mary Magdalene's collection. Sam Eisenstein fell in love with its glorious sound and was able to purchase it from his friend before it was lost from his reach at auction.

Many of the books that Betty Eisenstein seeks are children's books (especially pop-up books), many of which she recalls reading as a child.

Old Building, Paris (for Sally)
by Richard Bunkall (1953-1999)
Wood, wax, oil and plaster

Painters Sally Storch and Ray Turner hang this sculpture by Richard Bunkall in their Madison Heights colonial home. Bunkall, who was Storch's husband and Turner's closest friend, died from complications from ALS in 1999. Storch talks about this extraordinary work of art: *"Building a family, working hard and selling his paintings, Richard never did these sculptures – there are twelve in all – with the intention of selling them. He loved architecture – really, he was in love with buildings all over the world. This was a complete labor of love. He did every bit of this in his studio, carving the wood piece by piece, with no assistant. The building he modeled this on is on the Left Bank in Paris, and when he showed this piece, he put a tiny tape recorder playing Edith Piaf hidden inside the sculpture. It was playing so softly that people could barely hear it, but it was there. I think six or seven of these architectural sculptures were sold; we have five in our collection."*

Got Cream?

"You know how you may not mean to be collecting something, but it just talks to you?" asks Sally Storch. *"Creamers talk to me – a lot."*

Above: Jean Bennett's husband, architect Robert Edward Bennett (1915-2003), designed the home she shares today with her daughter, Annaly Bennett, son-in-law Jared Crawford and grandson Miles. Jean bought this painting by Raimonds Staprans around the time Miles was born, in 1996. *"I always wanted a great modern painting in this modern house,"* she says. Staprans, who was associated with the Bay Area Figurative Movement and such artists as Wayne Thiebaud and Richard Diebenkorn, emigrated from postwar Latvia in 1947 and is recognized as an important California painter.

Top right: The presence of Ender Sezgin's native Turkey is felt throughout the home he shares with his wife, Catherine, and their two children. In this well-known painting by Bedri Rahmi (1913-1975), a folk artist is playing a *saz*, a long-necked lute popular in Turkey. Rahmi taught painting at the Academy of Fine Arts in Istanbul and is one of Turkey's first and most illustrious modern artists.

Right: Evren and Erin Sibel Sezgin, 9 and 7, stand in front of the portraits made of them at ages 6 and 4. Denise Monaghan, a Pasadena artist, neighbor and friend of the Sezgins, photographed the children and, from those photos, painted the portraits – a diptych, says Catherine Sezgin, which allows the portraits to be shown together or separately, should the Sezgins one day wish to give them to their children. *"Denise is not interested in making vanity portraits,"* says Sezgin. *"It is her vision and her art. It was most interesting, as Erin Sibel is a very reserved child, and at the time she looked very timid and almost brooding in every photograph. And all the pictures of Evren were very happy. But in the actual paintings, Evren looks more somber and Erin Sibel looks almost happy. I believe Denise's specialty is making the children's faces look timeless. It was a very thoughtful process, and I can imagine both of them looking this way when they are older."*

Funky Junk Farms

As a child, native Angeleno John Agnew loved to visit his grandparents and roam about looking at *"a lot of old stuff"* in their eleven-bedroom, three-story home on Gramercy Place in Los Angeles. The first thing he remembers collecting were ventriloquist dummies in the 1960s. He also loved animals and made terrariums out of old TV cabinets for his dozens of snakes and lizards. *"I may collect different stuff now, but I haven't changed since I was a kid."* He's owned more than 500 antique cars over the years, as well as 100 antique travel trailers, antique camping equipment, outboard motors, automobilia (gas pumps and signage), antique car parts and some African-American memorabilia. He sees pretty much all his collections as Americana, and this Americana sprawls over his large property (which he shares with his girlfriend, bead artist Yipsi Border), a former fish hatchery in Altadena that he has dubbed Funky Junk Farms. He has never been interested in collecting mainstream pieces, being far more drawn to things that are *"oddball and strange."* John says: *"You may make some money collecting the mainstream stuff, but the people dealing with them are just not that interesting. It is all about who has the biggest and the best, and that is not my motivation at all."* Having been at this a long time, interesting stuff seems to just come his way. *"Sometimes I drive down a street and get that feeling... I make a right turn and, boom, there's something great there."*

Growing:
at home

The idea that a person can blossom where planted might be the most American of notions. It reflects the stubborn determinism that anything is possible, that our fate is neither preordained nor sealed by what our parents were born into or able to accomplish in their lifetimes. The chance to spring forth and develop, while still a theory in some parts of the world, was shouted out when we declared our independence as a set of colonies, and has continued to be fused into our national psyche. Horatio Alger, Louisa May Alcott, Charles F. Lummis and even the Beach Boys pushed westward as the country's borders and opportunities expanded. Optimism, often laced with desperation, spurred transplants from across continents to expand their ideas of what they could – or must do.

Pasadena, our charming suburb of greater Los Angeles, was the destination of 391 such people in 1880, many of whom wished to bloom all year round in the sun. By 1900, Pasadena had been a bona-fide city for fourteen years, and word had gotten out to come, if even just for the winter. The population of bootstrappers was a little over 9,000 at the turn of the last century. By 1910, 30,000 lived here. During this time culture took root in the form of the Pasadena Playhouse (1917), the Rose Bowl (1922) and the Grace Nicholson Art Museum, now the Pacific Asia Museum (1926). Counted in public works were the Colorado Street Bridge (1913), the expansion of Route 66 on Colorado Boulevard, the Arroyo Seco Parkway (1940) and the U.S. Army's purchase of the Vista del Arroyo hotel for use as a World War II hospital facility, which brought GIs to town, many of whom liked what they saw and settled here after the war. By 1950 Pasadena was home to not only 100,000 inhabitants but also lots of lovely architecture and thriving light industry. JPL started growing after Caltech's original "rocket boys" were encouraged to leave the campus (intact, please) and fire their explosions way up in the Arroyo. By 1958, they had created the first U.S. satellite, Explorer I, in response to Sputnik. By the 1960s smog and a shabby downtown encouraged an exodus that wasn't reversed until the 1980s, when Pasadena Heritage, formed in 1977, helped shepherd the area's robust revival.

Even when setbacks occurred, growth and change continued. President Garfield's intellectual wife, Lucretia, a former schoolteacher and independent thinker who opposed Prohibition, retired to South Pasadena after her husband's assassination. Mud Town was renamed Watts in 1900 for Pasadena realtor C.H. Watts, who owned a ranch there. The Rose Bowl's first African-American football player, Fritz Pollard, led Brown University to victory over Yale in 1915, and in 1922 organized the first all-star interracial NFL game. In the 1940s, pneumonia forced the retirement of the inventor of the "boom mike," film director Dorothy Arzner, who went on to teach filmmaking at the Pasadena Playhouse and UCLA, in addition to directing Joan Crawford in 50 Pepsi-Cola commercials. Retiring to South Pasadena with his wife was Henry Dreyfuss, the celebrated industrial designer and ergonomics pioneer who developed the J-3 Hudson 20th-century locomotive, the John Deere Model A tractor and the "Princess" phone, for America's teenage girls.

Pasadena and her neighbors continue to move forward as people continue to come, filling the condos and apartments that have sprung up over the last decade. High-density housing and mass transit are evolving here, as they are in many metropolitan areas, along with recycling incentives, conservation and restoration projects. Private and public groups are working to restore the Arroyo Seco, increase tree plantings in one of the leafiest cities in the state, protect historic buildings and add pocket parks for people and pets, all while remaining friendly. In many ways, Pasadena hasn't changed all that much in 150 years – it's just grown a few more blossoms.

– SG

Red, She Said

One of the first things Winslow (Winnie) Reitnouer will tell you is that she and her husband, Lynn, are not gardeners. But then they hired Heather Lenkin to design and install a red flower garden and a manageable vegetable garden, and now Winnie is outside every day. *"This is my first garden, and I love it!"* Winnie enthuses, like a kid in a candy store. *"Here's something I've learned. The more you cut the more you get. No one ever told me that before!"* She snips from sixteen rectangular terra-cotta pots planted in winter with snap peas, lettuces, sage, parsley and chives; summertime brings tomatoes, dill, zucchini, string beans, basil and peppers. *"I have the greatest hors d'oeuvres right here in the garden,"* says Winnie. *"I wrap our snap peas in red lettuce with a little bit of flavored cream cheese. It's wonderful, and so easy, believe me."*

Winnie and Lynn bought the San Marino house in 1964 and reared their children there. *"Our son started as a freshman in high school when we moved in, and now our grandson is a senior at Miami U in Ohio,"* she says. *"This has been a lovely location, very quiet, and we've been very happy here."* Except for one thing: the trees that the Reitnouers planted when they moved in. They wanted a shade tree, and when a gardener recommended the Cupaniopsis, also known as carrot wood, they planted not one, but three. They grew and grew and grew, producing pods that are painful to walk on. *"Barefoot? Not possible,"* sighs Winnie. *"Which was silly, because the children grew up swimming in the pool. We got to be good at cutting out all those horrible pods."* So the trees stayed, and they still provide excellent shade.

The time came two years ago for Winnie and Lynn to remodel the pool and Jacuzzi. *"I call the pool the world's biggest foot bath,"* Winnie says, laughing. *"I don't swim, but I'll put my feet in. I do love that Jacuzzi, though, for my shoulder."* As they discussed the pool, they decided it was time to reconsider the entire deck and back garden. *"We wanted to be able to use it, after all,"* says Winnie, *"so we found Heather and told her what we wanted."* The list included the color red (Winnie's favorite), ease of use and maintenance, and efficient water management. Heather recommended 36-inch-tall terra-cotta planters for the vegetables. *"That was a comfortable height for Winnie,"* says Heather. *"We wanted to bring the planters to her rather than the other way around."*

One other thing Winnie requested: daffodils. Lynn's favorite flower is a yellow daffodil. *"Heather planted 200 bulbs, and he was so surprised and pleased when they came up,"* Winnie recalls. *"Sweeps of color, yellow, and red and white, so beautiful. Heather breathed life into this garden."* Tucked among the bedded scarlet gerbers, geraniums, roses, camellias and primroses are white calla lilies, daisies, hydrangea, ferns and potted citrus. Winnie and Lynn are out there, too, having coffee or reading on the swing. How does her garden grow? *"It is glowing!"* she says. *"It makes me feel light. The garden increases a feeling of harmony with my surroundings. You want to get out there, put your mind in neutral, forget any aggravations, and enjoy."*

Winnie Reitnouer, above, has splashed her house and garden with touches of her favorite color, red. Sometimes she even gets her husband, Lynn, to stay in step with the red theme.

You Can Grow Home Again

Gardening is not about beginner's luck with attorney Michael Williamson. He grew up in Bristol, England, weeding and transplanting alongside his dad, who had an "allotment garden" plus a garden at their house. *"As children we were expected to help, and we eventually picked up the habit,"* says Michael. Allotmenteering, or community gardening as we know it, was also about planting from seed, cuttings or divisions, without benefit of buying pony packs from the nursery. Water was free, provided it was used carefully and not simply to hose the sidewalk. In this way, Michael learned to care for plants from the ground up, which has served him, his wife, Eileen, and their children quite well.

In the backyard of their San Pasqual home, the Williamsons grow a huge summer crop, including tomatoes, which can be fussy. Before planting eight varieties of heirlooms and hybrids, Michael prepares the raised beds with compost from the three bins the family keeps going year round. *"All the yard waste and trimmings go in the compost, as well as kitchen scraps,"* Michael reports. *"In the early spring I dig wheelbarrows full of it into the soil."* Once the planting is done, he supplements the heavy feeders, like the tomatoes, with a high-quality organic fertilizer. *"Then I rely on the compost and proper watering for the rest of the season,"* he says.

Another consideration is what to plant. *"Pasadena is a terrific place for growing just about anything, as long as it can survive the hot summers,"* Michael notes. So he's narrowed the selection to what works best: eggplant, corn, strawberries, beets, runner beans, five kinds of peppers, zucchini, rhubarb, arugula, lettuces and greens, along with a couple of dozen types of herbs, *"some of which I haven't figured out what to do with yet."* There's a mountain of basil at summer's end, and their four children help make *"the best pesto in the world."* The kids also love to eat strawberries and tomatoes right off the vine. *"Sam (age 13) especially loves the loquats and kumquats,"* says Michael. *"And unlike most folks in Southern California who have orange and lemon trees, we literally pick every lemon to make sorbet or lemonade, and we juice all the oranges for breakfast."*

With the garden providing "fast food," Eileen and Michael have come to accept slugs and snails. *"If I plant enough of what I want and they eat some of it, then that's better than noxious pellets. But beware any snail or slug when I have a pair of trimmers and a flashlight in the evening!"*

So where does a tiller go from here? For Michael, the path led to winemaking, which he's been pursuing for well over ten years. At first he bought high-quality frozen grapes in plastic drums. Eventually he and a friend started sourcing grapes directly from growers. Instead of choosing the grapes and the time of shipment, they get a call when their grapes have been harvested and are ready to be picked up. *"I quickly learned that buying the best grapes possible was worth it, as marginal grapes can never make more than marginal wine,"* he says. *"One of our best wines was a 2003 pinot noir from a Russian River vineyard. After hand-sorting and -crushing 1,000 pounds of great-looking fruit, we cold soaked it with dry ice for a week to extract color from the skins, did a short hot fermentation and racked it into a new French oak barrel. We racked the wine off the heavy lees only once, put it back in the barrel, then bottled it twelve months later without filtration. The wine was terrific – it held its own with many other high-end pinots."*

In the early fall, when the crush is on, the Williamsons have several late-night sessions with a handful of good friends who double as their winemaking crew, laboring in a converted garden-shed winery. *"Our little boys love to help with the pressing, and everyone has purple-stained hands for weeks afterward,"* Michael says. *"I like to think that someday our children's children will play in the dirt, plant seeds and pick the fruit with their parents, just like they do with us."*

Below: Some of Michael Williamson's growing real estate.

Opposite: Jack Williamson, upper left, in his family's backyard; Nick Williamson considers the big world at the end of his San Pasqual sidewalk; some of Michael's winemaking essentials.

Go, Green Man, Go!

In the tradition of British houses having names, Daniel "Rover" Singer and Cal Smith, co-owners of a unique, hand-built Altadena canyon house, named their home Green Man Lodge for, says Rover, *"the apparent fascination builder Louis Steinhauser had with the ancient symbol of man's face covered with leaves."* According to Rover, this represents the pagan symbol for the natural cycles of death and rebirth. *"There are many Green Man faces carved into the woodwork both inside and outside the house,"* he says. Steinhauser's wife and helpmate, Anita, contributed decorative hand-hammered copper relief works, which hang throughout the 1930s-era folk-art house.

Off the beaten path, Altadena has long been home to individuals who prize freedoms not afforded in neighboring Pasadena, such as relaxed liquor laws during Prohibition and septic systems in the 21st century. Preserving and restoring Steinhauser's folk-art masterpiece has become a quest for Rover and Cal. While none of the artist's tools were left behind, Rover does have a 1953 *Los Angeles Times* article that shows some of the fifty chisels Steinhauser used to carve hundreds of icons throughout the house. Four pieces of handmade furniture – two vanity chairs, a rocker and a chaise – remain, as does a hand-carved bathtub bench. *"We have some pre-decorated lengths of wood that were never installed,"* says Rover, *"as well as a carved sign for the family to whom he sold the house. He removed the section that said 'Steinhauser,' which we found and plan to restore."*

This page and opposite: The house that Louis Steinhauser built – and carved – by hand is a folk-art marvel now maintained by Rover Singer and Cal Smith.

Historic Growth

Carolyn and Craig Watson's children are the fourth generation of Craig's family to live in their 5,500-square-foot Oaklawn home, built in 1905 by developer G.W. Stimson. The Arts & Crafts Transitional building features a second-floor wrap-around balcony above a grand living room, which lends itself to performance or oratory. In fact, the house has enjoyed a long history as a gathering place for public causes. It was built by Judge Frank Cattern, a state legislator, and his wife, Clara Newton Cattern, a member of a prominent Pasadena family. *"Mrs. Cattern used the living room and second-floor balcony for many suffragette meetings,"* says Carolyn. Craig's grandparents, the Oechslis, bought it in 1945 and held many benefits for charity causes. They later passed the house on to Craig's parents, who sold it to Carolyn and Craig in 2001. *"We have deep roots here,"* says Carolyn, a landscape designer. *"It has been an ongoing passion of ours to revitalize this historic property."*

Household refurbishments during the Watsons' tenure have been numerous, ranging from the plumbing and electrical that are de rigueur for older buildings to extensive renovations to the grounds. Carolyn learned to garden as a child at her mother's side; she later went on to study horticulture and design. Although influenced by the materials and colors of Italian and French country gardens, Carolyn especially reveres Japanese gardens, which she has designed for clients. *"The Japanese garden is widely influential all over the world,"* she says. *"Everything is placed for a purpose."* At Oaklawn Carolyn carefully refitted pathways, designed and built wrought-iron and stone fencing, supplemented plantings based on foliage combinations, and refurbished the antique waterwheel, which operates now for the first time in thirty years.

After completing all this work, the Watsons found evidence, including old photographs, showing that the "canyon" garden, including the waterwheel and faux bois railings, was designed by Kate Sessions, the San Diego horticulturalist and mother of Balboa Park. An old friend of Clara Cattern, Sessions designed the flowers for the Cattern wedding in 1895, to which 1,000 guests were invited. *"I was thrilled to see many of my plant choices echoed the original plantings,"* says Carolyn. *"And in the front, I always felt there should be a center walkway. I was very happy to see an original photo showing that there was, in fact, a center walkway, almost in the exact place where I installed one."* Carolyn also redesigned the swimming pool, which was built by Craig's grandfather, Leonard Oechsli, in the 1950s, using much of the original brick and stone coping the patriarch personally gathered in Bouquet Canyon. She also preserved a working stone fireplace that Oechsli built by hand.

Not long ago, the house that Craig's grandparents often lent for public functions welcomed 65 people representing five generations of the Oechsli clan for a three-day reunion. *"We had a wonderful dinner with tables and candles in the canyon,"* says Carolyn. *"I think because of my time in Europe and New York, I love to have formal gatherings."* Christmas is an especially festive time for the house, with an annual holiday party, a sixteen-foot tree, wreaths in each window, and decorations that take an entire week to hang. In summer, Carolyn's northern Italian cooking is served al fresco, and meals are planned around the herbs and produce that she grows. As with all the previous owners, the Watsons lend their home to events supporting local causes, including the South Pasadena School District, the Church of Our Saviour and the Grace Center. *"I've never counted the number of days we have guests,"* says Carolyn, *"but from our children's study and play dates to dinner parties and the occasional gala, I would say that we entertain quite often. I want my guests to have a great experience, not just with food but with the whole environment."*

Below: Alexandra Watson is a fourth-generation resident of this 1905 home, which features a galleried living room that once hosted suffragette rallies.

Opposite: The Watsons' garden is rich with more than 100 years of horticultural history.

Retreating:
at home

The rooms in our homes provide space for overlapping tasks. We have phones, calendars and desks in the kitchen; we have TVs in the bathroom; and we spread out on the dining room table to wrap presents or sort laundry. After dinner, or even at some earlier time in the day, it is not uncommon for right-thinking people to retreat into quiet-time activities that can be done by only one. Reading. Daydreaming. Sleeping. Hallelujah! Quiet time in a world of busyness.

Retreat in battle may be a setback, a time to regroup over Plan B. In the business world, retreats are a time for the team to bond over a love of safety equipment and a tamped-down fear of rappelling. Retreating at home, at night, between crisp linens in your own bed offers a chance to recharge and fortify. By the way, the most popular American bed for counting sheep is the queen-size, followed by the twin, twin extra-long (popular in college dorms), Olympic queen, California queen (four inches longer and thinner, natch), sofa bed, water bed, platform bed, vibrating bed, air mattress, adjustable bed, futon, daybed, Murphy bed, pallet, bunk bed, basinet, crib, trundle and California, west coast or WC king, not to be confused with the WC (water closet), unless you're in a family bed, in which case it probably is a WC (water closet) king on occasion.

In classical times, Romans slept on a chamber bed, studied on a study bed and ate on a three-person *lectus discubitorius* while lying on their left side (the center spot was the place of honor). The final resting place began with a funeral bed, which was set atop a pyre. In Tudor England, luxuries like feather mattresses began to replace the straw mats of yore. Queen Elizabeth I's "progresses" around the realm defrayed the costs of the near-bankrupt monarchy as the clever queen invited the noble class to host her and her retinue. This encouraged the upper and rising merchant classes to curry favor with the queen and spruce up their bedding, because she was going to stay for a month on the host's farthing. When Elizabeth I was home, a flock of 1,000 geese provided down for the annual restuffing of the royal mattress.

Before electric lights and caffeine extended our days, the western world slept ten hours a night instead of our average seven. Anthropologists suggest that 5,000 years ago, people curled up for twelve hours per night, because life was physically exhausting and sundown was a good reason to stop repairing the chariot or tanning the hide. And even though Hamlet didn't do so well with retreating, which led to brooding about the Big Sleep, research over the last half-century has proven that the well-rested have better reflexes, improved memory skills and fewer accidents at work and on the road. Sleep aids in tissue repair, and dreams employ the unconscious to sort solutions for the next day's challenges. All of which could have curbed a certain Prince of Denmark's tendencies to snap at his mate or stab the guy hiding in the curtains. Experts, not all of them health-club proprietors, suggest that modern folk welcome sleep when the body, as well as the mind, is used each day. Exercise promotes nighttime sleep, which is vital to intellectual accomplishment and creativity.

In spite of, or because of, the levels of multitasking that go on in modern daily life, even the short daydream can provide a mental jumpstart. Taking stock, a pastime explored by famed sleeper Goldilocks, can be good for you, even if you have to try out several hammocks to find one that's just right for inventory-control purposes. A nook, a comfortable chair, a California queen, a spot under a tree, the corner where you stack lamp shades to put on your head at the next office party – all of them can be the right place to withdraw and draw a breath.

So now you know: The trick is to step back to allow the big picture into view. Take a break or a nap. Saw some logs. So that we may renew our spirits and our appreciation for all that we've made and done and have, it is good to retreat at home.

– SG

This page, clockwise from right: The Nunnery bedroom overlooks a tree-shaded canyon; a room of one's own at the Jansen-Gillums' South Pasadena cottage; Laura Davich in quiet study.

Opposite, left to right: Dogs relax in style in Norma and Gary Cowles's living room; a serene bamboo aerie in the Beck-Saland garden.

144

Sweet Dreams Past & Present

The Linda Vista house seen on these pages is so orderly it's difficult to imagine that it's not always an oasis of tranquility. The homeowner describes a bed frame upstairs: *"This was my husband's great-great-grandfather's bed, which was made especially for him, which they did in those days. You see how tall the legs are? This bed was built for the tropics,"* she says. *"It was originally a four-poster but somewhere along the line it was reduced. It's almost a full, but not quite. So I buy large sheets and tuck them under."*

Every object in the room, it seems, has a long history. The medals over the bed? *"Oh, yes, those were my father's. He was a British Army officer during the Sri Lankan independence in 1947. He gave his medals to his grandson, my son,"* who, this way, probably sleeps closer to his grandfather and great-great-great-grandfather than any other kid on the block. On a chest sits a black box inlaid with porcupine quills, also from Sri Lanka, and an old-timey telephone. *"My mother-in-law gave us the telephone. It was from a little store she owned, a car-parts sort of store, not very fashionable, but it was in a nice spot near the ocean. When the building was sold and the store dismantled, she gave us the phone as a memento."* Generations and continents intertwine through each room in the house. Another bedroom sports a teal and lime green bedspread against restful grey-violet walls. *"I don't have a decorator,"* she says. *"I do it myself. I looked at paint chips to pick the wall colors. I bought the silk for the bedspread in Hong Kong. And I had that funny little banner made for the canopy, too. I thought, 'Well, this is either going to work or it will be terrible!'"* she says with a laugh.

Most months out of the year it's cool enough for ceiling fans without turning on the AC. Even without humidity, the carved camphor-wood chest, which belonged to her mother-in-law, is the perfect place for saris. *"It preserves everything so well. Silk-eating moths do not bother me."*

The family used to visit Sri Lanka every two years, but now that the children are older they don't go as often. *"When we moved here, we thought it was so expensive to bring any of the old beds and trunks with us. We were afraid to spend the money. But I took the risk. Now it's not possible to even buy a piece of furniture for what we spent on shipping,"* she says. *"We kept these pieces, and I hope our boys will keep the things we pass on to them."*

This page, above: A green jolt of Hong Kong silk enlivens the Linda Vista guest bedroom; a comfortable chair in the library.

Opposite page, clockwise from left: Grandfather's carved teak bed, made in the tropics; solid wood bed frame brought from Sri Lanka; detail of turned-wood post; rattan couch and silk pillows make a retreat in the living room; antiques shipped with the newlyweds 30 years ago; an inviting upholstered settee.

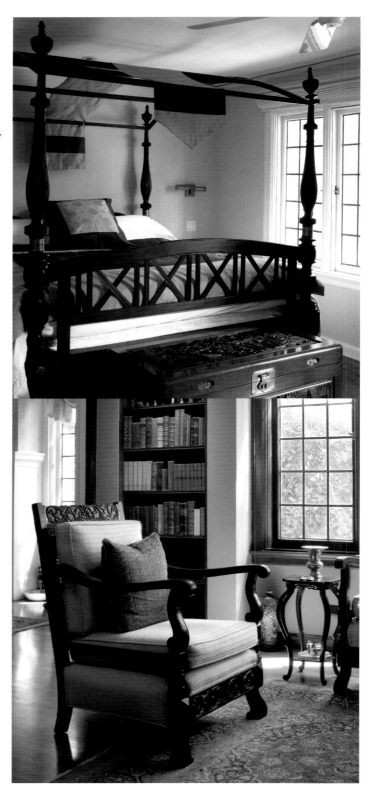

Left: Altadena's Funky Junk Farms is all about rustic comfort, as with this front-porch chair.

This page, clockwise from upper left: Porch chair in soft light for listening to the crickets; the Tripp-Ryans' bench swing in the palms; a ceremonial teahouse used for quiet retreats, play and birthday parties; Chris Jansen-Gillum and her son, Eliot, relax on their South Pasadena front porch; a leafy nook on the Watson porch; set a spell in the Madsen-Perry front-porch rockers; nap central in the Singer-Smith's hammock garden nook; the swing on the Madsen-Perry porch.

A Nap in the Shade

The Simpson Garden

Margie and Rick Simpson built their California colonial when their twins, now grown, were in high school. Margie, a landscape designer, has an office at home, and the garden is a workshop for her, a cloister for Margie and Rick, and a home for the wild creatures that commute between here and nearby Bailey Canyon. A swimming pool, spa and kidney-shape lawn anchor the back garden, buffered by voluptuous contoured paths and stuffed perennial beds that follow Margie's low-maintenance plan. Redwoods rim the one-acre property, screening nearby buildings.

"The top priority for the entire garden was lots of nooks and crannies," Margie says. To that end, she planned surprises around each curve: a rose allée to draw the eye from a back door, a snaking woods that leads from the guest cottage, and jolly little pocket planters along the pool hardscape before arriving at the lily pond. And those Adirondack chairs hiding just under the shade trees in the way, way back? *"As a matter of fact,"* she says, *"we call this spot our secret garden."* Like many of Margie's garden rooms, this one evolved organically. When the Simpsons first moved in, an old deodar guarded the lower forty. *"We were so happy to have that huge shade tree. We planned an alcove around it."* As it turned out, the tree was dying. The Simpsons worked to save it, building an elevated deck away from the roots. Ultimately, the tree failed, and Margie refreshed the gap with redwoods and Carolina cherry, underplanted with columbine and hardy geranium.

Now that the bones are established, what are the favorite activities here? *"This is a great place to read or have a cool drink,"* she says. *"And napping. Major napping takes place here."*

This page, clockwise from upper left: Adirondack chairs on a deck deep in the Simpson woods; a teak bench tucked into a shady nook; nap-friendly deck chairs at Simpson pool.

Opposite page: Peaceful nooks and crannies in the Simpson garden.

Miles Outstandish
What's on 10-Year-Old Miles Crawford's Nightstand (left):

Make Magazine (loves this techno DIY 'zine)
Ian Fleming's James Bond series, especially *Blood Fever*
The Zombie Survival Guide by Max Brooks
Hatchet by Gary Paulsen
Eragon by Christopher Paolini
Anything about model trains and rocketry

Favorite Bedtime Ritual: Miles and Mom read to each other for a bit, then Miles reads to himself.

Coolest Dream: When Miles was a little kid he dreamt he was riding on the back of a dragon or a flying dinosaur. Says Mom, *"He made a beautiful drawing of the flying creature. He's quite an artist, if I may say so."*

Dream a Little Dream
What Sophia Frank's Reading at 15 (right):

The Count of Monte Cristo by Alexandre Dumas
Balsac and the Little Chinese Seamstress by Dai Sijie
The Glass Castle by Jeanette Walls

Most Vivid Dream: *"I'm back at preschool and me and my friends are climbing on the wood jungle gym. Then this giant comes out, like the one from Jack and the Beanstalk, and he's chasing everyone and trying to step on them. We run toward this hedge, and through a hole that turns into a slide with all this greenery and flowers around it, like a fairy world. We all land, and I remember feeling really safe. Until the giant comes sliding down, too, and then I wake up. This was also a recurring dream that always went the same way and always ended in the same spot. So there it is, not very elegant, but I'm kinda tired."*

Kathryn Goes to College
In the Moments Before Leaving, a 17-Year-Old's Bedtime Reading (left):

Invisible Man by Ralph Ellison
The Beak of the Finch: A Story of Evolution in Our Time
    by Jonathan Weiner
The Claremont McKenna College Catalogue

Favorite Bedtime Ritual: Usually talking to a friend before bed. Or reading.

History Is Her Story
What Madlyn (right) Is Reading at 16 (When Not Studying for the AP History Exam):

Girl with a Pearl Earring by Tracy Chevalier
1776 by David McCullough
Lend Me Your Ears, Great Speeches in History
    selected by William Safire
A History of the American People by Paul M. Johnson
Founding Brothers: The Revolutionary Generation by Joseph J. Ellis

Favorite Bedtime Ritual: *"Madlyn is our early-to-bed person,"* says her mom. *"She always has been. At 8:30 or 9 p.m., you will find her in bed, reading."*

We are not retreating, we are advancing in another direction.
— Douglas MacArthur

Sorrow can be alieviated by good sleep, a bath and a glass of wine.
— Saint Thomas Aquinas

There was never a child so lovely but his mother was glad to get him to sleep.
— Ralph Waldo Emerson

I love sleep. My life has the tendency to fall apart when I'm awake, you know?
— Ernest Hemingway

I am accustomed to sleep and in my dreams to imagine the same things that lunatics imagine when awake.
— Rene Descartes

The Bunkall Boys & Their Books

What's on John's Nightstand at 14:

The Hobbit by J.R.R. Tolkien
Lord of the Flies by William Golding
Baseball's Most Wanted: The Top 10 Book of the National Pastime's Outrageous Offenders, Lucky Bounces, and Other Oddities by Floyd Conner
Of Mice and Men by John Steinbeck

What's on Henry's Nightstand at 14:

To Kill a Mockingbird by Harper Lee
Catcher in the Rye by J.D. Salinger
Watership Down by Richard Adams
My Personal Best: Life Lessons from an All-American Journey by John Wooden and Steve Jamison

What's on George's Nightstand at 13:

Harry Potter and the Order of the Phoenix by J. K. Rowling
Hood: The King Raven Trilogy by Stephen R. Lawhead
The Giver by Lois Lowry
The Hobbit by J.R.R. Tolkien

The Wee Quiet Hour
The Hermann Garden

Jane Hermann, a Colorado native, learned Pasadena gardening by rolling up her sleeves and doing. *"Start with the soil,"* she says, recalling her most satisfying home project, a rabbit garden. Jane and Carl moved to their Arroyo Tudor, greeted by sections of bony, dry, inhospitable dirt. She imagined perennials outside her office window and started mulching and tilling, while cultivating her brain with classes at the Arboretum. As an interior designer, a Digger, a hostess and a family woman who clears the calendar for visits from her children and Carl's, Jane doesn't get overly ambitious with her garden plans. *"I'm realistic about the garden and my schedule,"* she says. *"I'm not a lazy gardener. But there's just not enough of me to go around. So I make choices. I'm not set on seasonal color, and I don't fuss with that in front."* Delphinium, columbine and heuchera she now sees from her office window, *"when they're not eaten by visitors unknown."*

Foundation plantings have made mulching and water conservation easier. Planted pots spill with *"drifts of whatever's left over from various projects,"* she says. Before the day begins is Jane's favorite time in the garden. *"I'll sit in the alcove beyond the pool with my coffee and I'll think through my day. It is so, so quiet just before the sun comes up. A very loud bird joins me some mornings, then it gets quiet again and I watch the dawn."*

Previous pages: Scenes from the Hermann garden, including a wisteria-covered pergola, Jane's rabbit garden, and boxwood, callas and society garlic leading to the pool.

This page, clockwise from upper left: son Miles's bedroom in the Bennett-Crawford house; 13-year-old Lukas Frank's garrett retreat; Stella Frank's sleepover pals; Sam and Betty Eisenstein's carved headboard; a painted ceiling in the Watson home.

Opposite, clockwise from left: Daisy the dog catches 40 in the room she shares with 15-year-old Sophia Frank; Matthew White and Thomas Schumacher's curtained Castle Green sleep chamber; over the river and through the Doughertys' woods; Mark Puopolo and Chris Mullen's fainting couch in their Garfield Heights Victorian; an inviting daybed in the Davich home.

STAY!
at home

We're crazy about our pets. Why wouldn't we be? We're only human, after all, and our species has been domesticating and cohabiting with other species for a long, long time. How do we know this? Because there are scientists who research these things – and here's where we get to mention a way-cool job that only very few of us will ever get to drop into a dinner-party conversation: *"So your son is a dentist – how interesting. My daughter is an archaezoologist."* (Or you can switch it to zooarchaeologist – whatever works for you.) For our money, this is the hybrid scientific enterprise upon which Indiana Jones should have hung his dusty fedora. Sure, Indy had those Nazis and the Holy Grail, but, egad, man! It was an archaezoologist in 2004 who discovered that though we've long attributed the domestication of cats to the Egyptians, circa 2000 BC or so, Kitty's ancestors had actually taken up residence in the best Neolithic homes in Cyprus in 7000 BC – 5,000 years earlier! It was even further back in time – 15000 BC – that Rover's wolfish predecessor wised up, started loitering around the campfire, and stopped trying to bite the hand that fed it. And here's a tidbit to gladden the heart of the pet owners who have been heard to say, Rover thinks he's a cat, or Fluffy acts just like a dog: Well, duh! It turns out both cats and dogs are descended from a common mammal of the family *Miacidae*, which died out as many as 60 million years ago, but not before branching out into the families *Canidae* and *Felidae*, from which evolved our beloved dogs and cats.

This ancient human connection to animals extends beyond the cats and dogs that are our most common housemates today: Between 10000 and 4000 BC, the goat, sheep, pig, cow, chicken and horse were domesticated as pets and/or livestock. And while we thank our ancestors for all the hard work we know this must have entailed, how about a shout-out to our cave-painting cousins who were the first to tackle the sweetly dangerous work of beekeeping sometime around 13000 BC.

We bring our pets into our homes with a generous heart, and when the time comes, we grieve their loss deeply. If we're lucky, they are with us for a long time: The average – not maximum, mind you, but average – lifespan of a dog, not taking particular breeds into consideration, is about thirteen years; for a cat, especially if indoors most of the time, we're looking at fifteen years. That's more than long enough to establish themselves as genuine members of the house.

Lately, I've taken to referring to my pets as my distinguished colleagues, as in, *"I would be honored to have my distinguished colleague from His Favorite Spot on the Bed join me for a walk in the Arroyo,"* or, *"I'm sure my distinguished feline colleague is well aware that when I yielded the floor, I had no intention that that was what she planned to do on it."* But at seventeen years old, she retains her gorgeous fat tail and soft grey coat, and pill that she may be these days, I recall her fondly as a junior ball of fur, when she could chase a flashlight beam almost to the top of a door jam forever, and fetch Lego helmets like nobody's business, and provide hours of entertainment for our son and the little boys who were always here to play. I'll make you a friendly wager: Find me someone from that

other House of Representatives who has provided that kind of pleasure for that many years to his or her constituency, and I'll clean up after him as well. Well, what do you know – I win.

Ladies, gentlemen – some great Pasadena pets.

– JAG

This page (clockwise from right): Daisy waits for her nightly sleep-mate, 15-year-old Sophia Frank, in Sophia's room; Frankie protects one of owner Milo Reice's paintings; Molly in Karen and Ed Miller's Japanese garden; Sammy sleeps in style in Heather and Harvey Lenkin's master bedroom; Sylvie knows the comfiest spots in the Frank house; Scout can keep an eye on the Storch-Bunkall family from this perch on the living room sofa.

Next page, left: The Dutch door on Christine Madsen and Steve Perry's front porch makes it easy for Rajah to greet guests; Tigger stalks the Jansen-Gillum backyard in South Pasadena.

160

Left page: Jane and Carl Hermann's dog, Blossom, is a thoughtful gal who prefers to keep her front paws in a graceful second position.

Above: Hershey the chocolate lab settles in on the mocha leather sofa in Mark Puopolo and Chris Mullen's Garfield Heights Victorian; Heather Lenkin's always-watchful cat, Satchmo; Sammy likes the cool shade by master Paul Thomson's log-cabin office in Altadena.

Above right corner (clockwise): Elvis promises not to get his white fur on the Beck-Saland's purple couch; Augie, one of Jeremy Cowin and Dana Hursey's two dogs; Kitty Face keeps an eye on Jack Williamson and his breakfast; Sam and Betty Eisenstein's buddy, Zeke.

Right: Yellow lab Zooey and Labradoodle Gabby are thrilled when company comes to the grand Bertram Goodhue home they share with Norma and Gary Cowles.

This page, clockwise from top left: Margie and Rick Simpson's border collie mix, Moosie, keeps an eye on any errant tennis balls that might find their way into the pool; Gwen Babcock's dogs, Lacy (left) and Hobart, keep her company while she gardens; the Funky Junk Farms pack, from left to right, are Louie, Weezer and Festus.

Next page: Jordanne Dervaes tends to a flock of chickens and a pygmy goat at her family's compact urban farm, Path to Freedom.

Saving the World:
at home

Movements and trends do not spring wholly formed. They evolve over time, in response to events and situations. Environmental activism, for example, has been many years in the making, and may well have germinated in the late 19th century, when reactions to the Machine Age prompted a call to nature. Conservation and physical fitness jogged in the same circles, with the west coast's John Muir and the east coast's Henry David Thoreau leading the warm-ups. Mass production of bicycles and the epidemic of Spanish influenza made health a topic of national conversation. Writer Wallace Stegner said that national parks were "America's best idea," open to all and preserved for future generations. Who better to use those parklands than the Boy Scouts and Girl Guides, who jumped the pond to teach us how to tie knots and pitch tents, so that by the 1960s, crossing the Alps with Julie Andrews and Christopher Plummer seemed like a perfectly feasible idea.

Okay, so we've established that there was long a trend in the air. Even so, someone has to pick up the neighborhood gauntlet, or we'd never have cookie sales in the supermarket parking lot, and you can forget about your chance to sing in lederhosen. Often the doing starts with a party of one. The enthusiasm of that one person spreads, and before long, universities and local governments are acknowledging the need for, say, parks, or nontoxic surroundings, or recyclable products, or pesticide-free food.

Is it civic duty or moral fiber that calls a person to action? Or, as our friends from Madison Avenue know full well, is it advertising that gets people up off the couch? All we know is that in Pasadena, lots of people do good things every day. They put trash in the proper receptacle instead of throwing Burrito Express wrappers out the car window. They pick up after their dogs, they drive to the San Fernando Road facility to dispose of hazmats, and they return their library books on time, or at least pay their fines without making a fuss.

Sometimes citizens emerge who hear a different message and do more heavy lifting than the rest of us think is required. Rarer yet are those few who are modest while serving. They don't beat their drum right in your ear, mainly because they're too busy rolling up their sleeves to get the work done. The work of bettering our world. Saving the world, while we're busy eating a fish taco from Gerlach's. They live among us, go about their business, and do good works, because that's what they're made of. We submit but a few examples of these people for your edification and inspiration, while you finish your taco.

– SG

They Made Arlington Garden

You drove by this lot on Pasadena Avenue at Arlington Drive for years before noticing that it has taken a new shape. It was an abandoned lot, but lately, it looks kind of like a little arboretum. Say, what's with all those trees? And mulch, fountains, pathways… what's going on in there?

Glad you asked. Pasadena natives Betty and Charles McKenney are only too happy to field questions about the three-acre Caltrans lot they've shepherded into Arlington Garden. The garden is designed around its use of, and respect for, water. Betty seems to be here full time, having recently retired as a manager in technology services at Caltech. Charles, an attorney, is the first to say that Arlington Garden exists because, *"Betty had a vision. She made this happen."* In one of those chicken-or-egg moments, the couple forgets which came first, their Arlington Drive condominium in July 2002 (after a brief attempt at retirement in Santa Barbara) or the community-garden project they accepted at the urging of city council member Steve Madison. No, it was the condo first, they remember – the steering committee meetings came at the end of 2002.

Mulching and fencing started two years before the first trees were planted, in July 2005: six olives, one pistache, two sycamores, two chilopsis and three peppers. Which means the McKenneys devoted two and a half years to organizing before the community saw a single bit of positive progress.

Both Betty and Charles have a long history of working with volunteer organizations. Which is another chicken-and-egg question: Are the McKenneys practical because they volunteer, or do they volunteer because they are practcal? Betty served with parent associations in their children's schools, in the Junior League and on the board at Mothers' Club Community Center in Pasadena. Charles served two terms on the Pasadena City Council (reminding voters with packets of Forget Me Not seeds), as well as with the Santa Monica Mountains Conservancy and the Pasadena Civic Conference Center, and he's now on the Parks and Recreation Commission. *"Charlie has always been a very helpful advisor,"* Betty says. *"He's given me guidance on how to be a good board member and work with a group."* Charles offers, *"You have to have something to work with, and Betty has it. She saw this garden."* Both agree it has been easier to commit their energies to making a public park now that their kids are grown. So they are mortal! And they are also quick to share the credit with others.

Before Madison drafted the McKenneys, Caltrans had granted a five-year lease on the property while waiting for progress on the 710 corridor. The neighborhood had spoken for passive development of the lot, vacant since the Durand mansion was razed in 1961. But what kind? Athletic fields? Dog park? Tot lot? Betty and Charles gathered an advising committee, and Betty kept coming back to Jan Smithen's book *Gardening under Mediterranean Skies* as a template. Landscape architect Todd Holmes got excited when he heard Betty and Charles's hybrid notions about what might work in a new kind of city green: paths, shade, trees, succulents, fields of lavender, water elements, orange groves. These would be Mediterranean gardens: French here, Italian here, Aramaic there. *"Todd went to Cal Poly Pomona and recruited students to work on concept designs,"* says Charles. *"We gave them all our ideas, and they came back with great drawings, pictures of what it really could be, for us to take to the city.*

"Nobody knew if this was going to work, because this was a new kind of park we were proposing," says Charles. The city folks didn't say no, even if they were skeptical. *"The possibility of how beautiful it would look is what kept us going,"* says Betty. Their practical and friendly determination convinced others. George Brumner from the Mediterranean Garden Society came on board. Nancy Long from the Metropolitan Water District worked on a grant to pay for signage. Jan Smithen helped recruit a landscape designer, Mayita Dinos, who drew working plans. Jan Muntz from Pasadena Beautiful Foundation and Randy Finch from Pasadena Water and Power started helping on a regular basis. *"People were saying, 'It sounds like a great idea, but I'm not convinced,'"* remembers Betty. *"So we'd forge ahead with another step. Then they began to see what we were doing, which made them more willing to help."*

In five years a public garden with 300 established trees has grown on a once-scrubby lot. Welcoming split-rail fences frame the newly planted Cherokee roses, an ode to the rose hedge that stretched from Orange Grove to Pasadena Avenue in the early 20th century. Pedestrians visit regularly, some with dogs, who are welcome. Wildlife shows up at the fountains. The garden progresses with new swaths of iris (Betty's sister sent 100 bulbs, divided from her own garden), and volunteers collect California poppy seeds to direct their germination. There are raised vegetable and demonstration beds, occasional how-to lectures and continuous weeding, pruning and mulching, which Betty does herself or oversees. And the watering! To conserve precious H2O, it's still done frugally by hand, requiring more than 40 hours a week, until funds are in place for an irrigation system.

The McKenneys' willingness to volunteer so much time has kept the garden alive. And it couldn't have happened at all if they didn't live next door, because there was no money for sprinklers. *"Eventually, the garden won't rely on us. It will become institutionalized,"* says Charles. *"That's good, for the life of the place. We're just happy to have been a part of the process."*

Adds Betty, *"Even if this all goes away tomorrow, I can see 300 trees where there were eleven when we started. I feel good about that."*

Right: Scenes from the developing Arlington Garden.

Following spread: Some of the "rooms" of this Mediterranean garden-in-progress, which emphasizes California-friendly plants; Betty and Charles, upper right, inspect the garden's progress; the piece of iron grate, upper right center, is among the remains of the Durand mansion, which was razed in 1961.

On the Path to Freedom

Call the Dervaes family busy. Others have called them modern homesteaders, eco-pioneers or urban pioneers. The City of Pasadena calls them Outstanding Recyclers, awarding them several commendations for negating their carbon footprint. They run a micro-agriculture business (that is, a farm) out of their modest home, which has been recognized as one of the most eco-friendly businesses in Los Angeles, producing a 6,000-pound annual harvest from a one-fifth-acre backyard. They use a combination of high and low technologies, including solar cells, simple metal solar ovens, greywater irrigation and homemade biodiesel. Oh, and brains and muscle.

Jules Dervaes and three of his adult children, Anaïs, Justin and Jordanne, operate Path to Freedom, an amalgam of entities all rolled into their shingled cottage on a tree-lined street. The goal is better stewardship of the land, which seems to be hard-wired into Jules. Originally from Florida and New Orleans, he was a homesteader in New Zealand in the 1960s, and when he brought his young family to Pasadena in the '80s, he had long known that materialism wouldn't define his life. A former schoolteacher who was educated as a mathematician and engineer, Jules was influenced by his gardening grandfather and his Belgian ancestors, who cultivated a sense of beauty and order through keen hand-eye coordination (think Belgian lace). The care and precision with which Jules constructs raised vegetable beds and tomato trellising, or the way he coils a hose at the solar shower, is mathematical but playful. This guy's an artist. And to talk to him, well, he's got a good sense of humor, too.

The Dervaeses' hobbies and their habits of gardening, adapting and improvising combined with a thoughtful use of money to converge into one grand and rippling idea: that they could do a variety of things better. Jules, the mathematician, taught his children to draw graphs and record data to track the number of flowers, tomatoes or blueberries that could be grown within certain parameters. *"Using these numbers, I thought it would be pretty neat to chart our progress as we worked to multiply our harvest,"* Jules says. *"The kids were challenged early on to think about what we could do if we wanted to."* At that point, gardening was still a hobby. Adds Anaïs, *"We always did the typical recycling things, like only running full loads of laundry, turning off lights when leaving a room and using greywater."* By the '90s they progressed to growing food organically; they now produce enough to feed themselves and supply several high-falutin' restaurants.

"At dinner, we're always having conversations about global events or political movements," says Anaïs. *"And Dad will say, 'How can we do this differently?'"* That's Jules, the schoolteacher. *"So we go off and research the topic and come back to dinner the next night. Dad says, 'Give me what you've got,' and we dissect, strategize and figure out a way to improve the situation."* So the Dervaes family decided, according to Anaïs, *"The way we live will be our path to freedom, our proactive protest."* In order to make the world a more hospitable place, they would slow down and live in a simple fashion.

Simple, but not in a vacuum. The Dervaeses are hardly insulated from the world. School groups visit, their gardens were a demonstration site for Pasadena's 2007 "Green City" tour, and from time to time they offer public events and lectures to share what they're learning. They maintain an incredible web site (pathtofreedom.com), thick with practical information that's beautifully and graciously displayed, with more links and progress reports on their urban "experiment" than you could fit into an electric car. *"You know, seven years ago, when I started journal postings on the internet, there were almost no references to urban homesteading,"* says Anaïs. *"Now it's urban-pioneer this, urban-homestead that. I guess we're part of history,"* she laughs. *"Trends like the 100-mile diet are popular now, which is really funny to me. We've got the 100-foot diet! Our food's really locally grown."*

The Dervaes family isn't standing on a soapbox. For one thing, there's too much work for standing around. *"I don't believe one size fits all,"* says Anaïs. *"This is the path we've chosen. But we're not saying there's only one answer for everyone. We're improvising all the time, and there's always room for improvement."* So they are up early every day, tending their chickens, ducks and goats, minding unusual weather patterns that could destroy a summer heirloom tomato crop (it's happened) or freeze the winter's entire salad planting, costing three weeks of growing. The Dervaeses are conscious that they are tied to the land, the weather and their neighbors in Pasadena and across the globe. And they are fortifying those ties slowly, with purpose.

Facing page, clockwise from top left: The Dervaes men use this solar-heated shower all summer long; bamboo stalks make exceptionally tall and compact vegetable tepees; herb and vegetable beds fill the central yard.

Following spread, left page, clockwise from upper left: The Dervaeses often cook their entire dinner in this clay oven; a baby chicken from the flock; Jules used chunks of the former concrete driveway, which was sacrificed for growing space, to create a concrete flower interspersed with plantings; modern versions of ancient ollas are buried next to plants so slow-seeping water can keep roots moist; Jordanne and Jules at work in the foreground, with Justin and Anaïs in the background.

Right page, clockwise from upper left: Justin feeding the pedal-powered grain miller; scenes from the "farm"; you can work off that shake before you drink it with this bicycle-powered blender; Jules and Justin filtering used restaurant vegetable oil to create fuel for their Chevy Suburban; Jules providing pedal power; Jordanne cradling a pygmy goat.

Reusing It, Not Losing It

Each generation has its campaigns and causes that bring people together. Long ago we learned that loose lips sink ships, that we should buckle up for safety, and that only we could prevent forest fires. Recently we heard a dynamite slogan from a preschool teacher that could well be a motto for today's recycle-reuse era. Miss Gloria only half jokingly wanted a bumper sticker that proclaimed, "I Brake for Styrofoam," because that's what she does after Lunch Bunch five days a week. She pulls over to the curb to collect such treasures as the packaging from somebody's new TV or computer. Schools have been keeping little hands busy making useless knickknacks out of popsicle sticks and old magazines since George Washington cut down a cherry tree and had to have a parent-teacher conference. And boy, those teachers come up with some brilliant and easy ways to recycle: picture frames out of the bottoms of clear plastic cups, birthday crowns from fancy-fold newspaper, a candle made out of the nubs of old crayons melted into a jelly jar. If you're not sure how to proceed into the recycle-reuse era, ask that lady who just pulled over to pick up a pile of styrofoam if she has any good ideas. Or move on into junior high and develop some research skills. Kids aren't the only ones who can learn about ways big and small to save for a planet's rainy day, not to mention ways to make the planet less toxic. Here are just a few practical solutions our neighbors employ.

The Art of Recycling

Joseph Shuldiner creates art (pictured above) by recycling both manmade materials and those found in nature. A sculptor and fiber artist, Shuldiner was influenced very early on by the tactile expression of such found objects as bark and twigs. *"I made '60s art as a kid – macrame, weaving, ornaments out of leaves,"* Shuldiner says, laughing. *"I took every class offered at Barnsdall Junior Art Center."* His work was always about nature. The L.A. native was influenced, too, by his family's practical approach to art as a vital component of daily living. Grandfather Joseph Lewitzky, the Depression-era painter, reared his family in a Socialist Utopian community in the Mojave. *"My parents were not artists themselves, but they were free thinkers,"* he says. *"They certainly appreciated art and artists."* And his aunt, Bella Lewitzky, was a renowned dancer and choreographer.

Shuldiner's recent work includes ephemeral textiles with arboreal matter sewn or laced in, as well as delicate patterned rugs woven from plastic grocery bags. *House Beautiful, New York, Los Angeles* and *Interview* magazines have featured his work, which has has been shown in solo and group shows in national museums and galleries since the 1980s.

As they remodeled their house, he and partner Bruce Schwartz took great pains to find old hardware and fixtures from antiques stores and through the internet. An old bathtub that was rescued from a salvage lot fit perfectly. And no oil-based paints or MDF were allowed – water-based paints and nontoxic, sustainably harvested woods were de rigueur for this green remodel.

Left, clockwise from top left: A compass rose points the way to thoughtful garden usage; a bell in the Whitford garden pays homage to Pasadena's Spanish heritage; John Reveley created this walkway out of recycled bits from his wife's ceramics studio; why buy new when a recycled stove can be so fabulous?

Below, clockwise from top left: An old-fashioned cloche allows seedlings and cuttings to grow sturdy; bamboo is a renewable wood source; recycling bags are poised by the back door for easy access; these 1940s wall ovens came with the Nunnery house; they thought twice before condemning them to the landfill, and they work, says Ed, "*perfectly.*"

I'm Green, Now That You Ask

When Catherine and Ender Sezgin were planning their remodel in 2003 (see kitchen, far left), the only toxicity or renewable-resource information available was on the internet. *"It was impossible to get info from the salesperson on the green aspects of the building materials they sell,"* says Ender, amazed. *"They had no knowledge of the health effects of their products. So I did a lot of research to select materials."*

Here's what Ender settled on: All plywood used in wall panels is marine grade, with cherry and maple veneers applied with exterior-grade glue. Plywood for other uses is exterior grade, which has little or no formaldehyde. He used no waffle board, interior-grade plywood or pressed wood (which typically contain formaldehyde), and the other wood products he selected, including flooring, contain little to no formaldehyde. All hardwood flooring was nailed, not glued. (And they clean their woodwork with Bona, a nontoxic product.) Electrical wiring is in metal conduit, to lessen ElectroMagneticField (EMF) effects. The crushed-rock aggregate is all natural and new. Says Ender, "This may not be environmentally sensible, but suppliers would not guarantee that the crushed concrete wasn't contaminated. Knowing that some of the recycled concrete used for aggregate comes from old gas stations or contaminated facilities didn't make me feel safe about using it." Finally, the Sezgins haven't used any herbicides, pesticides or fungicides in the garden since 1998, when they purchased the property.

Resource Guide

This quirky and by no means comprehensive guide offers up the results of an unscientific survey – basically, things such as antiques stores, appliances, designers and even takeout restaurants favored by the *At Home* homeowners. We also list some of the homeowners themselves for their professional relevance to the subject matter. We also did a little borrowing from our earlier offering from Prospect Park Books, *Hometown Pasadena*.

Antiques & Collectibles

Depression Glass
www.depressionglass.net

Thomas R. Field American Antiques
1127 Mission St., South Pasadena
626.799.8546, www.thomasrfieldantiques.com

Froebel Gifts
www.froebelgifts.com

Funky Junk Farms
323.309.8087, www.funkyjunkfarms.com

Bruce Graney & Co. Fine Antiques
1 W. California Blvd., #615, Pasadena
626.449.9547, www.brucegraneyantiques.com

Susanne Hollis Inc.
230 Pasadena Ave., South Pasadena
626.441.0346, www.susannehollis.com

Pasadena Antique Center & Annex
444 & 480 S. Fair Oaks Ave., Pasadena
626.449.7706, pasadenaantiquecenter.com

Pasadena Architectural Salvage
30 S. San Gabriel Blvd., Pasadena
626.535.9655, www.pasadenaarchitecturalsalvage.com

Pasadena City College Flea Market
Hill St. & Colorado Blvd., Pasadena
pasadena.edu/fleamarket

Roger Renick Fine Arts & Antiques
696 E. Colorado Blvd., #17, Pasadena
626.304.0008, www.renickarts.com

Rose Bowl Flea Market
1001 Rose Bowl Dr., Pasadena
323.560.7469 rgcshows.com

Souvenir Building Collectors Society
www.sbcollectors.org

Yoshino Japanese Antiques
1240 E. Colorado Blvd., Pasadena
626.356.0588

Appliances & Kitchen Supplies

Dacor
www.dacor.com

Fisher & Paykel DishDrawers
U.S. Appliance
877.628.9913, www.us-appliance.com/fispaydis.html

Bob Smith Restaurant Equipment
1890 E. Walnut St., Pasadena
626.792.1185

Sub-Zero Refrigerators
www.subzero.com

Thermador Appliances
www.thermador.com

Viking
www.vikingrange.com

Wolf Range Company
www.wolfrange.com

Architects, Designers & Architectural Services

Annaly Bennett Interior Design
annaly@annalybennett.com

Michael Berman Limited
323.933.0220, www.michaelbermanlimited.com
Interior design and furniture

Blue Studio: Liza Kerrigan
www.bluestudiosite.com
Architectural & interior design

Jeremy Cowin Appraisals
626.794.5988 www.jwcowin.com
Real estate appraisal

Johnny Grey Kitchen Design
888.640.7879, www.johnnygrey.com

Michael Halpern Designs
323.646.1751
Interior design

Aleks Istanbullu Architects
1659 11th St., Suite 200, Santa Monica
310.450.8246, www.ai-architects.com

Georgie Kajer
Kajer Architects
626.795.6880, www.kajerarchitects.com

Moule & Polyzoides
80 E. California Blvd., Pasadena
626.844.2400, www.mparchitects.com
Architecture & urban planning

Jean Maurice Moulene
beauxartsdesign@aol.com
Architecture & design

Mark Puopolo
310.926.8662, mark@hamrickhousepalmsprings.com
Historic restoration consultant

Marmol Radziner & Associates
310.826.6222, www.marmol-radziner.com
Architecture & design

Carolyn Watson
cmwdesign1@yahoo.com
Interior & garden design

Matthew White
White Webb
165 Madison Ave., New York
212.889.2900, www.whitewebb.com
Interior design

Artists

Elaine Carhartt
www.elainecarhartt.com
Commissioned murals & sculptures

Angela DeCristofaro
www.beznic.com
Commissioned paintings

Jennifer Frank
joanoufrank@mac.com
Mixed media & photography

Lynne McDaniel
626.794.5500, www.lynnemcdaniel.com
Commissioned paintings, murals & trompe l'oeil

Denise Monaghan
denisemonaghan.com
Commissioned portraits of people & pets

Kamran Moojedi
kmoojedi@verizon.net
Commissioned paintings

Milo Reice
milocalifornicus@aol.com
Commissioned paintings

Joseph Shuldiner
www.josephshuldiner.com
Mixed media & graphic design

Sally Storch
storchbunkall@sbcglobal.com
Commissioned paintings

Ray Turner
storchbunkall@sbcglobal.com
Commissioned paintings

Faith Wilding
faithwilding@cs.com
Commissioned paintings

Books & Magazines

American Bungalow
www.ambungalow.com

American Bungalow Style
by Robert Winter & Alexander Vertikoff (Simon & Schuster)

American Horticultural Society A to Z Encyclopedia of Garden Plants
by H. Marc Cathey (DK)

An Architectural Guidebook to Los Angeles
by David Gebhard and Robert Winter (Gibbs Smith)

Frank Lloyd Wright: An Autobiography
(Pomegranate Communications)

Illustrated Dictionary of American Architecture
by Ernest Burden (McGraw Hill)

Neutra, by Barbara Lamprecht (Taschen)

Sun Drenched Gardens: The Mediterranean Garden
by Jan Smithen (Harry N. Abrams)

Western Garden Book
Sunset magazine editors (Sunset Books)

Building Biographer

Tim Gregory
timgregory@sbcglobal.net

Construction Materials, Decor, Tile & Woodwork

Architectural Detail
299 N. Altadena Dr., Pasadena
626.844.6670
Antiques & salvage warehouse

Arroyo Hardwoods
2707 E. Foothill Blvd., Pasadena
626.304.0021, www.arroyohardwoods.com

Bisazza of Italy
www.bisazza.com/usa
Mosaic glass & ceramic tiles

Boen
www.boen.com
Renewable wood flooring

Bradbury & Bradbury Art Wallpapers
707.746.1900, www.bradbury.com

Medite Ecologique
www.medite-europe.com
Formaldehyde-free cabinet products

Mission Tile West
853 Mission St., South Pasadena
626.799.4595, www.missiontilewest.com

Tap & Tile
3191 E. Foothill Blvd., Pasadena
626.405.0098, www.tapntile.com

Furniture & Cabinets

Stranger Furniture
626.405.0927, www.strangerfurniture.com
Sustainable, organic furniture and cabinetry

Garden Resources

Arlington Garden
Pasadena Ave. & Arlington St., Pasadena
626.441.4478

Creative Arts Group
108 N. Baldwin Ave., Sierra Madre
626.355.8350, www.creativeartsgroup.org
Annual garden tour

Descanso Gardens
1418 Descanso Dr., La Canada
818.949.4200, www.descansogardens.org

Huntington Botanical Gardens
1151 Oxford Rd., San Marino
626.405.2100, www.huntington.org

L.A. County Arboretum
301 N. Baldwin Ave., Arcadia
626.821.3222, www.arboretum.org

Path to Freedom
www.dervaesgardens.com, www.pathtofreedom.com

Rose Information
www.helpmefind.com/roses

Hardware & Fixtures

Crown City Hardware
1047 N. Allen Ave., Pasadena
626.794.0234, www.crowncityhardware.com

Liz's Antique Hardware
453 S. La Brea Ave., Los Angeles
323.939.4403, www.lahardware.com

Pasadena Lighting
731 E. Walnut St., Pasadena
626.564.1112, www.pasadenalighting.com

Restoration Hardware
127 W. Colorado Blvd., Pasadena
626.795.7234, www.restorationhardware.com

Historic Resources

Castle Green
www.castlegreen.com

City of Pasadena
www.cityofpasadena.net/history

Pasadena Heritage
www.pasadenaheritage.org

Pasadena Museum of History
www.pasadenahistory.org

Landscape Architects, Designers & Contractors

Rick Button, ASLA
626.403.1875

C & K Landscape Design
818.353.7030, www.candklandscapedesign.com

Mayita Dinos Garden Design
610.838.5959, www.mayitadinos.com

Heather Lenkin, ASLA
626.441.6655, www.lenkindesign.com

Picture Perfect Construction
626.303.5902, www.pictureperfectconstruction.com

Gabriela Yariv Landscape Designer
310.301.7234, www.gabrielayariv.com

Organizer, Home/Office

Sally Miller
626.578.1620

Photographers

Jennifer Cheung
www.jennifercheungphotography.com

Dana Hursey
626.345.9996, www.hursey.com

Steven Nilsson
www.stevennilsson.com

Visiting Pasadena & Environs

Hometown Pasadena
www.hometown-pasadena.com

Pasadena Convention & Visitors Bureau
www.pasadenacal.com

While Your Kitchen Is Being Remodeled

Casa Bianca Pizza Pie
160 Colorado Blvd., Eagle Rock
323.256.9617

Europane
950 E. Colorado Blvd., Pasadena
626.577.1828

Gerlach's Grill
1075 S. Fair Oaks Ave., Pasadena
626.799.7575

In-N-Out Burger
2114 E. Foothill Blvd., Pasadena
310 N. Harvey Dr., Glendale
800.786.1000

Julienne Fine Food
2649 Mission St., San Marino
626.441.2299, www.juliennetogo.com

Los Tacos
1 W. California Blvd., Pasadena
626.795.9291

Nicole's Gourmet Foods
921 Meridian Ave., South Pasadena
626.403.5751, www.nicolesgourmetfoods.com

Pie 'n Burger
913 E. California Blvd., Pasadena
626.795.1123, www.pienburger.com

Raffi's Place
211 E. Broadway, Glendale
818.240.7411

Vertical Wine Bistro
70 N. Raymond Ave., Pasadena
626.795.3999, www.verticalwinebistro.com

Wine

Cellar Tracker
www.cellartracker.com

Gerlach's Drive In Liquors
1075 S. Fair Oaks Ave., Pasadena
626.799.1166

Mission Wine Shop
1114 Mission St., South Pasadena
626.403.9463

Opposite page, left to right: One of Angela DeCristofaro's paintings in her studio in the Barcelona apartments; George Ellery Hale's library in the Hale Observatory.

Index

Opposite page, top to bottom: In the planting beds at Path to Freedom, Pasadena's groundbreaking urban homestead; the woodwork at David and Judy Brown's Greene & Greene home represents the best of Pasadena's bungalow craftsmanship.